SO-CAL Speed Shop's
How to Build
HOT ROD CHASSIS

Timothy Remus

Wolfgang
Publications

First published in 2013 by Wolfgang Publications Inc.,
P.O. Box 223, Stillwater MN 55082

ISBN 13: 978-1-935828-86-0

Printed and bound in U.S.A.

On the Front Cover: Main: The SO-CAL Speed
Shop '32 Ford roadster uses today's techniques
with the best of yesterday's esthetics to produce a
hot rod for the 21st century. David Fetherston Inset:
The SO-CAL roadster's simple but effective chassis
uses traditional hot rod suspension designs to
provide safe, reliable, and comfortable operation.
Eric Geisert, courtesy of Street Radder Magazine

On the Back Cover: Main: The SO-CAL Speed
Shop offers complete hot rod chassis, like this one
for a '32 Ford. It features "step boxed" rails, a
tubular K-member, an I-beam axle with hairpin
radius rods, and ladder bar rear suspension. *SO-CAL*
Bottom left: The angle of your hot rod's shock
absorbers or coil-over shocks is very important to
how the finished car will ride and perform. Here,
Neal Letourneau uses an angle finder to properly
locate the coil-over shock mounts on this '32 Ford
pickup chassis. ***Top right:*** Modern IFS for your
hot rod is just a kit away ... this '32 Ford frame is
getting a new front crossmember that will mount
Mustang-II derived independent front suspension.

Library of Congress Cataloging-in-Publication Data
Remus, Timothy.
How to build hot rod chassis / Timothy Remus.
    p.cm.
Includes index.
ISBN 0-7603-0836-5 (pbk. : alk. paper)
    1. Hot rods-Chassis-Design and
    construction. I. Title.

TL255.R4523 2000
629.28'786—dc21   00-059437

Contents

Acknowledgments

It's like I alway say: You can't do it alone. Writing a book is kind of like building a car. No matter how good you are you still need an upholstery guy, and help with the paint, and of course there's alway the wiring to worry about.

In this situation I have to start by thanking Pete Chapouris for opening the SO-CAL shop to me and my camera. Tony Thacker, Pete's media man, acted as master of ceremonies while I was there, arranging photo shoots and interviews and providing a variety of good ideas. Everyone within the SO-CAL organization held out the welcome mat, including foreman Shane Weckerly and front end expert Jim Sleeper.

Nearby shops like that of Todd Walton and Jerry Kugel took up where the SO-CAL crew left off. Todd took the time to show me how a set of rails is converted into a complete SO-CAL frame, while Jerry and sons allowed me to do a sequence that shows how a typical Kugel front suspension system is installed.

The other two chassis builders who need mention here include an amateur and a pro. The nonprofessional is Chris Shelton, the young man who impressed Pete Chapouris by assembling his frame in record time so he could drive the car to a local event. Neal Letourneau is the professional, who with John Keena's permission, encouraged me to stop by and photograph every step of their chassis building proces.

For help with the wheels chapter I need to express my gratitude to Phil at PS Engineering and Alan at Budnik. And finally I need to express a collective thanks to everyone in the industry—all the staff and ad agency personnel who helped by sending images and information on the rails from Deuce Factory, the frame from TCI (Total Cost Involved), the brakes from ECI (Engineered Components, Inc), the axle from Super Bell, the motor mounts from Chassis Engineering, and all the rest.

Good Books Don't Die

Despite the dire predictions for "The Book," there are still some that just won't die. When I wrote this book for MBI almost fifteen years ago, I never dreamed this simple how-to book would have a second life. Publisher/author contracts of that era stipulated that when a title went out of print all rights reverted to the author. And in the years since How to Build Hot Rod Chassis was first published I've moved up the food chain. From author to publisher under the Wolfgang Publications banner. Thus I was lucky enough to acquire the publishing rights to this title from MBI, and put it back on the shelf as part of Wolfgang's catalog.

The most important thing here really isn't the money, though that helps of course. The most important thing about this situation is the fact that I've been given an opportunity to keep good technical information alive and available to a whole new generation of hot rodders, street rodders and motorheads. Because camber is still camber and brakes still work on the same principles of physics they did fifteen years ago. Better yet, SO-CAL Speed Shop is still a very viable entity and a leader in their industry. As I said the first time, I'm grateful to Pete and the SO-CAL crew for all their help.

It turns out that at a time when the half-life of most products, from books to music to apparel is about ten nano-seconds, How to Build Hot Rod Chassis lives on.

Introduction

Big projects get pretty overwhelming. For me, these projects become manageable only when they're broken down into a series of smaller subprojects. Instead of being overwhelmed because I decided to build a whole cabin, I focus only on the materials needed to build the basic structure. What do cabins and cars have in common? Nothing. Except that both are large undertakings best approached with the right mixture of planning, knowledge, enthusiasm, and money. When it came to the cabin, I worked on the site first, then the foundation, and finally the task of putting up the walls. Almost a year after hauling the first load of stuff out into the country, I had the basic structure finished.

Building a car is no different. If you dwell on the cost and complexity of your dream car, it will never be built. Better to start on the foundation of the car (called a chassis in this case) and focus on that. Even the job of building a chassis can seem intimidating, or at least confusing, with all the suspension and brake options currently available.

The goal of this book is three-fold: First, to educate you as to what's available in terms of complete frames and components. Second, to help you understand the procedures needed for assembly of those components. Third, to convince you that you *can* build this car, by yourself, in a reasonable period of time and for a reasonable amount of money.

The book is broken down into nine chapters that parallel the chassis-building process. First comes planning, then the construction or purchase of the bare frame. Next, the purchase and installation of the front and rear suspension. Before you're finished you need an understanding of hardware and plumbing, and some understanding of where the engine and transmission should mount.

For a look at how they build a SO-CAL chassis or a Kugel Komponents suspension, I've provided step-by-step sequences from a variety of shops. Sidebars and interviews allow you to share in the wisdom of men like Pete Chapouris and Ken Fenical. At the very end is the sources section, an industry listing of everyone mentioned in the book.

I've tried to provide the information you need to build a hot rod chassis. The rest is up to you.

Preface:

A Short History of the SO-CAL Speed Shop

by Tony Thacker

Unlike many such tales, the story of the SO-CAL Speed Shop is not one made up by some clever marketing types; it's a true story of friendship, hot rods, and the need for speed.

Our story begins on March 22, 1922, in Los Angeles, California, with the birth of Alex Xydias. Although his father was a prominent producer of silent movies, Alex's childhood was fairly normal, and like most young boys, he naturally gravitated toward automobiles. His first hot rod was a '29 Ford roadster with a milled head and a chopped flywheel. He paid for the car with part-time earnings and drove it to Fairfax High School.

After graduating, Alex worked in a gas station and saved enough to buy a '34 three-window coupe, which was followed by a beautifully customized '34 cabriolet, originally found in the lower basement garage at the Ambassador Hotel in Los Angeles. In 1940, Alex joined the Wheelers, a Southern California Timing Association (SCTA) club located in Norwalk, California. Then, in 1942, his life, like that of so many young men, changed when he joined the Army Air Corps, serving as a B-17 engineer.

According to Alex, "All we talked about during the war was cars, and once, when on furlough, a friend took me to a street race out in the San Fernando Valley. I was really surprised at how fast the cars ran, and I got the idea to open a speed shop."

On the day of his discharge, March 3, 1946, Alex opened the first SO-CAL Speed Shop, on Olive Avenue in Burbank, using borrowed money.

Alex Xydias opened his first SO-CAL shop in 1946 right after his discharge from the war. One year later he moved on to shop number two, seen here, in Burbank, California. The streamliner is the work of Alex and Dean Batchelor. Mercury powered, it ran 210 miles per hour in 1950!

Among the fast cars to come out of Alex's shop was this lakester, powered by a V-8 '60 Ford flathead.

Pete Chapouris and the car that put Pete and Jake's on the map: the California Kid. *Tony Thacker*

"I really struggled to keep it going," says Alex. "Sometimes I made less than $100 a month, but the hard work paid off. When my one-year lease was up, I moved the shop to 1104 South Victory Boulevard in Burbank where I put up a Sears, Roebuck and Co. prefab two-car garage.

The hot rods that bore the SO-CAL Speed Shop logo ran in pretty fast company. For example, a V-8 60-powered belly-tank lakester clocked 136 miles per hour in 1948 and appeared on the cover of the January 1949 issue of a fledgling *Hot Rod* magazine. This early success was quickly ratified when Alex teamed up with legendary auto enthusiast and author Dean Batchelor to develop a purpose-built streamliner. Powered by an Edelbrock-equipped Mercury V-8, the 'liner ran 210 miles per hour in 1950. The following year Alex and some racing buddies formed the SO-CAL Speed Shop Racing Team and built the first hot rods to go 160, 170, 180, and 190 miles per hour. In 1952, *Mechanix Illustrated* magazine voted the SO-CAL gang the number one racing team.

While fast cars continued to run under the SO-CAL banner, Alex embarked upon another endeavor: documenting auto racing events. He filmed everything from Bonneville to NASCAR, including Pikes Peak, Indy, and the 24 Hours of Sebring. "It was hard work," says Alex. "I'd spend hours behind the wheel getting to an event which I'd then have to film, before spending hours printing and editing the film."

Meanwhile, in the adjoining San Gabriel Valley town of El Monte, another California Kid was bitten with the hot rod bug. Born of a hot rodding father,

A good cigar to smoke and a great hot rod to drive, does it get any better than this? *Tony Thacker*

Pete Chapouris started "cruisin' the boulevards" with his friends around 1955. They'd start at the El Monte In-N-Out restaurant on Valley, go straight west to Farmer Boys, then out on Colorado to Bob's in Glendale before turning around and going east to Henry's in Arcadia. As had been the case during Alex's childhood, this too was an influential time for a young man.

Pete's first hot rod was a Model A coupe atop Deuce rails. A $200 Chevy V-8 was mated to a Packard transmission at Blair's Speed Shop, and Barris Kustom was paid $10 to reverse the wheels. Like most enthusiasts, Pete went through a string of cars, wheeling and dealing his way up market until he could afford a brand-new '61 T-Bird.

For Alex, the speed equipment business had undergone many changes. The flathead Ford, in

Built with help from Pete Eastwood and Jim "Jake" Jacobs, the Limefire car helped garner attention for Pete shortly after the sale of Pete and Jake's in 1987. *Tony Thacker*

The Pete Chapouris Group built many fine hot rods, but some of their most significant work involved restoration of historically significant cars, including one that may be the first "highboy," Doane Spencer's roadster. *Tony Thacker*

which the SO-CAL Speed Shop specialized, was no longer the hot rodder's favorite, and small firms like Alex's were under increasing pressure from the "big boys." The final straw came when Alex's right-hand man at the shop, Keith Baldwin, left. Alex closed the doors in 1961.

Although Alex's filmmaking was doing well, he accepted a position as editor of Petersen Publishing's *Car Craft* magazine in 1963. He stayed with Petersen for 12 1/2 years, transferring to *Hot Rod Industry News* where he later became publisher. While there he also served as director of the annual Petersen Trade Show, which eventually became the SEMA (Specialty Equipment Market Association) Show—the third largest trade show in the United States. After leaving Petersen, Alex went to work with partner Mickey Thompson, organizing the SCORE off-road equipment trade show.

At the time, Pete Chapouris was working as a product development technician at Clayton Industries, a dynamometer manufacturer. During his tenure there he met Mike Hoag, who left Blair's Speed Shop to form M&S Welding with Sherm Gunn, building dragsters. Pete wanted to work for M&S and consequently took welding classes at night until they gave him a part-time job. In 1971 he left Clayton and went to work at Blair's.

A member of the Vintage Tin Hot Rod Club, Pete began work on a chopped '34 coupe that would have an impact on not only his life but also the hot rod world. Finished in traditional black with flames, the coupe was photographed for the cover of the November 1973 issue of *Rod & Custom* along with a similarly chopped canary yellow coupe built by Jim "Jake" Jacobs. The two rodders hit it off and decided to start a small hot rod repair business in Temple City, California. Then came the call from Hollywood, specifically Howie Horowitz, producer of the hugely successful Batman series. He wanted Pete's car for a made-for-TV movie called *The California Kid* starring a young actor named Martin Sheen.

The California Kid put Pete and Jake's Hot Rod Parts on the map and the pair ran a thriving business. Because of their innovative style and seat-of-the-pants marketing savvy, Pete and Jake took the hot rod business out of the backyard and into the mainstream. Meanwhile, in 1982, Alex was inducted into the SEMA Hall of Fame.

Pete and Jake's was eventually sold in 1987, the year Alex retired, and Pete went to work as vice president of marketing at SEMA. Having been instrumental in the formation of the Street Rod Equipment Association (SREA), the job was a natural and Pete became a driving force in the transformation of SREA into the Street Rod Marketing Alliance (SRMA), a council of SEMA. Pete was also inducted into the SRMA Hall of Fame.

Pete has never been a stuffed shirt or desk-bound kind of guy, and when it came time to move on from SEMA, in 1990, he formed an alliance with Bob Bauder called Syntassien. Among other exciting projects, the pair completed a pair of high-profile Harley-Davidsons known as "HogZZillas" for Billy F. Gibbons of ZZ Top. The friendship with Billy resulted in numerous projects.

Syntassien was a long word but a short-lived company. Pete had a bigger vision and in 1995 he opened the Pete Chapouris Group (PC³g) at 1357 East Grand Avenue, Pomona, California. Under Pete's direction and with the help of his team of craftsmen, PC³g quickly evolved into one of the world's premier hot rod shops, garnering gallons of magazine ink for the cars it built.

One of the first cars that PC³g was involved in was the restoration, for Bruce Meyer, of the Pierson Brothers' 1934 Ford coupe, which led to an enduring association and the eventual restoration of Alex Xydias' SO-CAL belly tanker, also for Bruce.

Cover-quality cars were produced by PC³g with prodigious speed; the list included Don Simpson's Killer 1934 Chevy coupe, several cars for Billy F. Gibbons (including a 1936 Ford three-window coupe and "Kopperhed," a 1950 Ford coupe), and an extended-cab 1929 Model A pickup for Chuck de Heras. However, the crowning glory in PC³g's body of work was the restoration of the Doane Spencer 1932 Ford roadster for Bruce Meyer. Built by Doane in 1948 to compete in the infamous Carrera Panamericana Mexican road race, this car has an impeccable pedigree. By installing Lincoln drum brakes, 16-inch wheels, and raising the engine,

Full Circle, Alex and Pete in one of the new SO-CAL roadsters. *Tony Thacker*

A perfect merger. Together Alex and Pete have over 80 years of hot rod experience, more industry contacts than anyone alive, and a shared vision for a new SO-CAL that combines the best of both old and new. *Steve Coonan*

exhausts, and gas tank to increase ground clearance, Doane unwittingly spawned the classic "highboy" look that enthusiasts the world over continue to emulate more than 50 years later. It's also a look that won the hearts of the Pebble Beach judges, winning the inaugural Pebble Beach Historic Concours d'Elegance Hot Rod class. It also won the perpetual Dean Batchelor Memorial Award for Excellence.

The win at Pebble Beach would be a fitting end to a chapter, but not before Pete and his friend Alex were selected as two of the Top 100 Most Influential People in the high-performance industry and, as such, were inducted into the *Hot Rod* magazine Hall of Fame in 1997.

Our story doesn't end there, though. For a while Alex had been working behind the scenes with Pete Chapouris to resurrect the famed SO-CAL Speed Shop. On November 21, 1997, that dream became a reality, and PC³g changed its name to SO-CAL Speed *Shop to begin another* chapter in this on-going hot rod history.

Chapter 1

Know What You Want

Though it sounds too simple, you need to know what this new car is going to look like, how it's going to be used, and how much it will cost in dollars and hours to go from a sketch on the wall to the finished car.

Planning for the new hot rod is the most important step in the whole project. Ordering parts, bolting the wheels onto the frame to make it a roller, lowering the engine into place; all those steps might be more exciting, but the task of deciding *which* wheels and *which* engine is ultimately more important than buying or installing the parts themselves.

At SO-CAL and at most professional shops, the planning comes before anything else. As Pete Chapouris states in the interview that follows, "The first thing we do is come up with a concept for the car."

You need to know not only the budget, but how you intend to use this new vehicle. Do you want it to be really fast, or just look fast? The nostalgia trend is in full swing; anyone trying to build a car that looks like it came from another era needs to lock in that era and get all the details just right. The hot rod world of today encompasses a

SO-CAL likes to have a rendering of any car they build, before starting on the project. The rendering ensures that the customer and the shop "see" the same vehicle, and also gives the customer something to hang on to until the real thing arrives. *Thom Taylor*

wide variety of car types and styles. The good news is that you can build a back-to-basics rod, a nostalgia rod, a billet rod, or your own interpretation of what a modern hot rod should look like. The bad news is that it can be hard to pick exactly what you want from such a vast menu.

Many professional shops use a rendering or formal drawing to cement the concept for the car. If customers do not have an exact idea of what they want, a designer like Thom Taylor or Chip Foose is hired to work through a series of sketches until the customer says, "that's it, that's the car." Then the sketch is used to make a full rendering, complete with paint color and graphics.

In the case of your plan for the new hot rod, start by clipping magazine photos of your favorite cars, or build a photo-file of cars with the look you're after. You don't have to build a clone of what you see at a show, but if something has the "look" you're trying to achieve, it makes sense to define and use the essential parts of that look. The builders of the stretched Deuce pickup seen farther along in this book took some frame-to-ground clearance measurements from cars they found at the various car shows. They used those figures along with some photos from magazines to provide a starting point for the rake angle and ride height of their truck.

During the early part of this process, pay attention to things like the body proportions of the cars you study. Note whether the top is chopped, the rake, the tire sizes front and back . . . these are all critical dimensions. As one experienced builder explained to me, "what's important is the proportions of the car, not just the dimensions."

In other words, you need to pay attention to the relationships between the parts of the car. How much you chop a top has a major impact on the car's looks, partly for some not-so-obvious reasons. The relationship between the height of the top and the mass of the body is terribly important, and helps define the look of the car. When you chop the top, or section or channel a body, you've made a big change in this essential relationship. This is your car, you can do anything you like. Just be sure to think first and cut second.

The more unusual the hot rod, the more important the rendering becomes. Working from the customer's wish list, the artist will do a whole series of similar concept sketches until the customer identifies one particular sketch as "the one."

Designed for Robert Wolf, this radically restyled '46 Buick is the work of Eric Aurand. With a car like this, detailed renderings become an essential guide to the builder. *Eric Aurand*

Design Like a Pro

Plenty of hot rodders and custom car builders sketch their projects before starting. Some of those sketches are nothing more than doodles on a napkin. To formalize the process and make it a better prediction of what the new car will really look like, you can borrow some ideas used by professional designers and car builders.

First, start out with a stock side view of the car. This can be a photograph or an image clipped from a magazine. The important thing in either case is that it be a straight side view without any distortion. Now, take the image over to the copy machine and make some big blowups and a whole series of

This chassis, seen under construction further along in the book, is stretched 3 inches from the stock dimension. Whether the one you build is bone-stock or modified in some way, you need to have a detailed drawing of the chassis before the project begins.

To eliminate the guesswork and save money too, SO-CAL offers this complete kit, including their chassis and a steel Brookville body. *SO-CAL*

copies. Next comes the fun part. With scissors and tape, cut off the top and raise or lower it to your heart's content. Study the effect of a little more or less cutting. This method will also help you predict how much you need to add to the middle of the roof as you cut the posts and lower the lid.

You can use the same methods for lowering the car, trying different rake angles, or the impact of channeling the car down over the frame. When you've got the look you want, make some enlargements of the finished product and hang them on the refrigerator. Then check and see how they look in a week. You can even use colored markers to try different paint colors or graphics packages.

For the more computer literate among us, a scanner and PC can make the whole process easier. Scan the original into the computer, make some copies of the resulting file, then use a software package like Adobe Photoshop to lower the lid or change the rake angle. This might be your opportunity to finally learn how to use the PC you bought

the kids for Christmas. Who knows? This could turn into a family project.

The methods don't really matter. What does matter is the end product. Just like the big shops, you want an image of the finished car—one big enough that you can stand back and appreciate the proportions and overall look of the car. This image will be the visual blueprint for the project. It will help keep you excited about the car when energy or money run low and it becomes hard to stay involved. The image taped to the refrigerator or tool box will also help to keep you focused. When a new set of wheels or a new fad shows up in the magazines, you won't be tempted to begin modifying the plan for the car.

Concrete Planning Steps

You need to know more than just what the car will look like. Obviously you need to know how much the car will cost as well. Figuring out the true cost means being brutally honest about how much of the car you can build yourself.

We all like to think we're the world's best mechanics—that there isn't anything we can't do, or can't learn to do. If pressed we could rebuild the space shuttle before the next launch. However, if this new car is going to get finished before the end of the next millennium, you may have to be more honest about both *your mechanical* abilities and your available free time.

We all have to farm out some of the work. Only a small percentage of us are qualified to do finish paint work, and even fewer would attempt to do any upholstery work. Part of the budgeting process involves breaking the assembly of the car down into various subunits. Will you buy a complete crate engine, for example, or rebuild the one sitting in the back of the garage? If you intend to rebuild the engine, you will need a budget for outside machine work. And if the machine shop is going to grind the crank, bore the block, and fit the pistons, maybe it makes sense to let them do the finish assembly of the entire engine. For a little help deciding exactly which engine best suits the new ride, take a look at chapter 8.

On a personal level I'm a big believer in "do it yourself," whether it's a plumbing project in the house or installing ball joints in the daily driver. In the real world, though, most of us run out of time. The classifieds are always filled with project cars and street rods that didn't get finished. Those projects started off as someone's dream, but somewhere along the line they turned into nightmares. The idea is to *finish* the car, and in order to do that you need to keep a certain momentum. Something needs to get done every month, preferably every week. By farming out some of the jobs you could do yourself, more total work gets done during a given period, and the slow progress of turning a sketch on the wall into a finished vehicle is more likely to stay on track.

At SO-CAL they use elaborate planning forms that list every part on the car along with the price. In fact, the Chassis Builder's Checklist is available on their Web site. Another series of forms lists outside labor for things like sandblasting, polishing, upholstery, paint, chrome, glass cutting and installation, and even the final detailing. Before the project starts they know exactly how much it's going to cost, how many hours of labor are involved, and how many of the operations will have to be performed by outside shops.

In the same way you can make a list of all the parts and their cost, and all the necessary labor operations. Now break out the labor jobs you can't or won't do yourself and get cost estimates. The planning should include time estimates as well. How long will it take you to assemble and paint the frame, and how long will it take the chassis shop to narrow the *Ford 9-inch* rear end? Try to schedule the various labor operations so things dovetail. For example, you can't make the chassis a "roller" until that rear end is finished and painted.

It's Gotta Be Real

The planning and estimating needs to be as realistic as possible. If you underestimate either the time or money needed for the

project, it's easy to get disappointed when things take longer than needed or cost more than expected. Cost overruns can also play havoc with the family budget and destroy family support for the new hot rod.

Because the finish bodywork and paint are such a big part of the project, in terms of both time and money, some home builders finish everything but the body, assemble the car, and drive it in

The finished product of the rendering seen in this chapter. Considering what it costs to build a nice hot rod, you don't want any surprises when it's done. That's why planning is so important. *Tony Thacker*

Fred Fleet's roadster is another very successful car built by the SO-CAL shop—with help from detailed renderings done before any parts were ordered. *Tony Thacker*

Note the detail on the Fred Fleet chassis: the two-tone paint job, the neat routing of the exhaust and the gas lines. Remember, the chassis is the foundation for the car. *Tony Thacker*

primer for one year. This strategy does stretch out the time needed to truly finish the car, but it puts it on the road that much sooner.

The biggest advantage to this method is the fact that you can go out and have some fun with the car *now*, instead of one year from now. Back-to-basic hot rods always have a certain allure and seem to get more popular as time goes on. You don't have to tell them it's unfinished. Just paint it primer black (or gray) and drive it proudly to the local or national event. It also gives you a chance to "debug" the car easily—disassembling an unpainted car for repairs or adjustments is easier and less stressful.

The other advantage of this program is the fact that you allow the bank account to recover while driving the car in primer. When it comes time to pull the body off for that high-quality paint job, you can have the money already set aside in the savings account.

Speaking of Money

The topic of money brings up a short discussion of how you pay for this car. Too often home builders try to pay as they play. Just write a check for the frame, then the axles one month later, and

the wheels one month after that. While the long-term nature of most of these projects makes this type of financing possible, there's an Achilles' heel here as well.

The trouble comes when your need for something expensive coincides with a low point in the family cash flow. Then the purchase of the engine or tranny or wheels gets put on hold until funds are available. The project stops moving forward, your own attentions are drawn elsewhere, and before long the "new hot rod" is just that pile of parts over in the corner of the garage—the one you haven't put a wrench to in six months or more.

When you finish the car or buy a partly finished car and complete it, it will be worth a fair amount of money. Just look at the prices for nice street rods at a national event or in the back of *StreetScene*. Why not borrow money for the project and thus remove one more potential speed bump on the construction highway? Tell the banker it's a finished car, or borrow the money against the house, or take a loan at the credit union. Simply make sure you have a source of funds so that a monetary shortfall or a hiccup in your personal finances doesn't put the project on the back burner.

Things You Need

In addition to the rendering you need to know the dimensions for the car and the chassis. Though this is covered more in chapter 2, you need a working drawing of the chassis so you know where the firewall, axle centerlines, and body-mounting holes are.

Pete Chapouris feels strongly that anyone who is starting from a complete car should take the time to measure everything before blowing it apart. Even if you plan major changes, it's good to know how far the stock bumper was from the ground, and how much clearance there was between the frame and the concrete slab the car is parked on for the measuring session. Get out your camera and take some pictures, both close up and far away. If nothing else, these may be the basis for the clip-and-paste session mentioned earlier.

Disassembly

Though many new hot rods are built entirely from new parts, many of us are working from an existing car, finishing someone else's project, or rebuilding an old stocker. In either case the disassembly must come first and it should be done with caution.

Keep the camera handy and take plenty of photos both before and during the disassembly. They will prove a great aid when you try to put Humpty Dumpty back together again. Even if you don't intend to use all the old hardware, gather it into logical groupings and place each group in a large zip-lock bag with a label inside. If nothing else, the labels will help you sell or give those original parts to someone who needs them.

It's easy to just rip everything apart and then congratulate yourself for the speedy disassembly. The trouble comes later when you're trying to figure out which bolts hold the hinges to the body, or where the door handles are, or whatever happened to the trim pieces after they came back from the chrome-plating shop. A small investment in extra time spent during the disassembly will pay big dividends when it comes time to screw it all back together again.

Sometimes the simplest cars (or trucks) have the most appeal. This "ranch truck" 1929 Model A roadster pickup from SO-CAL uses steel wheels, straight yellow paint, and a subtle rake to create a package that's easy on the eyes. How much the hot rod will be driven has a major impact on the parts and finishes used on the chassis. *Tony Thacker*

Don Simpson's Killer Coupe is another of those cars that require careful planning and detailed renderings. Remember that underneath those great lines and that nice body is a chassis that holds it all together *and gives the car its stance.* *Steve Coonan*

The assembly—this is actually the second time Chris has assembled this chassis—starts with a SO-CAL chassis and various suspension components. This sequence is meant to show how a typical SO-CAL frame goes together, and does not exactly match Chris' description of the original assembly.

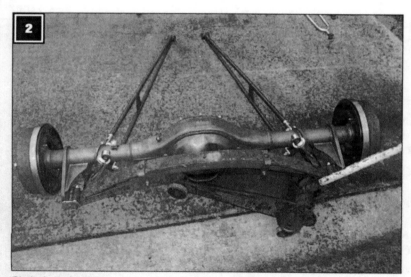

Chris bought the rear end housing from SO-CAL already narrowed and with the ladder bar brackets attached. The spring is a 1940-Ford-style spring from Posies. Once the spring is attached to the housing, the whole thing can be bolted up to the cross-member.

*A*s an In the Shop sequence for this first chapter, we've elected to show a typical SO-CAL chassis and how it goes together. The frame forms the foundation for a project owned by Chris Shelton. Still in school, Chris is working with a limited budget and assembling the car in the small single-stall garage behind his apartment complex.

This little section describes the way Chris outfitted his frame and stayed within a budget, and documents any troubles Chris had during the assembly.

The Starting Point

Chris started with a standard SO-CAL Deuce frame, though this one has a provision for a clutch instead of the more common automatic transmission (the difference in the two frames is covered in more detail in chapter 8).

Though most of these frames use the SO-CAL springs on both ends, Chris chose springs from Posies. In the rear, Chris used a 1940-Ford-style spring supplied by Posies and designed specifically for this frame and suspension. This spring came with reversed eyes and hidden sliders, so it looks as traditional as possible.

Chris reports that the assembly of the rear suspension and 1940 Ford spring did involve a fair amount of work. "It's hard to compress the spring to install it. I used 1 1/2-inch box tubing, longer than the spring, and a great big, 12-inch C-clamp to straighten out the spring against the tubing and make it long enough to install. I did this job alone but would never do it again without some help.

"I hung the rear end in the frame first, without the spring, just the rear end and the ladder bars hanging there. Then I compressed the spring and put it on the *rear end with the* shackles. Next I raised the whole thing up into position under the frame and bolted the spring to the center clamp assembly on the cross-member."

At the front of the car Chris used a 47-inch dropped axle from Chassis Engineering, primarily because it's a

With the radius rods already in place, Chris attaches the main leaf, before bolting on the rest of the leafs.

Here Chris shows us the hidden sliders, designed to reduce internal friction in the Posies front spring.

The complete assembly, a 47-inch forged axle with Magnum spindles and "drum" brakes from SO-CAL, before being bolted up under the frame.

With the frame on jack stands it's relatively easy to roll the axle assembly in underneath, and then start the assembly by first attaching the radius rods to the pivots on the frame.

The drums are really just covers for the SO-CAL disc brakes, and go on last.

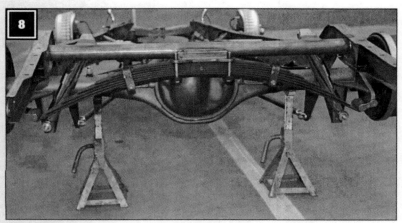

The rear spring bolts to a pad that's part of the rear cross-member. Some cars use a spacer between the frame pad and the spring to raise the back of the car.

stronger, forged steel design. Like the rear spring, the front spring is from Posies while the spindles are 1937 to 1941 Ford style from Magnum.

To assemble the front end Chris started with a bare axle, "Then I put the batwings and perches on. Next I installed the hairpins on the batwings (they only go on one way, the long side on the bottom, or the caster is way off). Then I slid the whole assembly under the frame and installed the bolts that go through the frame mounts and the hairpin rods. Then I attached the main leaf without the rest of the stack, and pulled it up into the mount and loosely clamped it all together." Chris does intend to use a Panhard rod on his Deuce.

"Then I set the frame at the approximate ride height and checked the caster with my protractor. I first measured the caster with the front end mocked up at approximate ride height without the spindles attached to the axle. I used the machined 'flats' atop the axle where the kingpins affix the spindles to the axle. Later I double checked everything with the spindles and wheels installed and the car at static ride height. For the final measurement, I measured using the flat portion at the very top of the kingpin flange that holds the felt seal in place.

"I adjusted the axle's caster from 6 to 10 degrees, just to make sure the spring wouldn't bind, and then I set it at 8 1/2 degrees. Next I bolted the rest of the leaves in with the main leaf, and installed all the hardware, like the headlight stands, the Pete and Jake's shocks, and a Vintique stainless spreader bar.

"For the brakes I used the SO-CAL-supplied hardware and instructions. Without the dustcaps on the kingpins, I slipped the backing plates over the spindles and installed the caliper flange brackets and polished stainless Pete and Jake's steering arms. I then assembled the hubs and rotors and secured them with safety wire. After inserting the bearings, I installed the rotating assemblies on the spindles with the washers and castle nuts. With the hubs and rotors installed I shimmed the calipers at the point where they mount, with the supplied washers, to center the calipers over the rotors. Finally, I installed the pads and inserted the fittings to adapt the SO-CAL hoses to

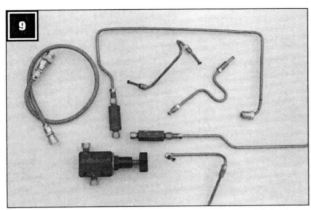

For brake plumbing, Chris used standard 3/16-inch double-flared steel lines. The nice thing about using these lines is the fact that they are readily available in a wide variety of lengths from nearly any automotive parts store.

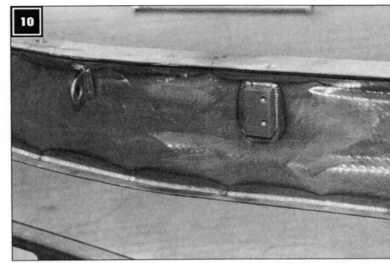

Where things like proportioning valves are to be bolted to the frame, Chris had heavier strap welded in place, then drilled and tapped. This same method was used to mount the gas filter to the right frame rail.

Here you see the proportioning valve mounted to the frame, and the SO-CAL-installed bracket where the hard line meets the flexible brake line that runs to the rear axle.

Small stainless clamps, held in place with Allen-head machine screws, keep the lines neat and securely in place.

the NPT threads in the Wilwood calipers. I then bolted the backing plates to the caliper flanges and installed the finned brake 'drums.' At this point I left everything finger tight, since I had to partially disassemble everything to bleed the brakes later on."

For plumbing, Chris chose not to use stainless brake lines. Instead he installed standard 3/16-inch steel brake lines from the local Pep Boys outlet. As Chris explains, "I used the steel lines because they're not nearly as expensive as the stainless lines. I also used the regular lines because I prefer an OEM-style inverted flare, which isn't possible to do with stainless [stainless lines require 37-degree single flares and AN fittings]. I suppose it's just a matter of preference, but I feel the advantage of the inverted flare's superior seal

outweighs the added labor of the additional flare—not to mention if I damage a line somewhere, the local parts stores carry inverted flare lines and fittings. For brackets I used the SO-CAL fittings which were already attached to the frame. For clamps I used aircraft-style stainless steel line clamps with stainless steel hex-head screws and washers. To fasten the clamps to the chassis, I drilled and tapped holes into the boxing plates."

The fuel filter is a standard AC brand filter available at any auto parts store, No. GF 62C. Chris welded 1/4-inch strap to the rear of the frame rail, then drilled and tapped that for mounting the fuel filter. The hard lines are 3/8-inch steel fuel lines, while the flexible lines are the style you can make up yourself. "For flexible fuel lines I used Aeroquip Teflon-lined stainless braided line," explains Chris. "The raw hose can be cut with a fine-toothed hacksaw, and assembled at home with common wrenches."

The fuel tank is from Tanks, Inc., and is a relatively new item. It has the stock reveal and shape stamped directly in the top just like an original 1932 tank. This tank has a fabricated bottom that allows for more volume but doesn't hang down any farther than a stock one. It attaches to the three stock tank-mounting holes atop the rear frame horns. Tanks also supplies the unit with a vented stainless cap, a cut-to-fit pickup tube, and a remote-mount aluminum vent. The tank also has provisions for a universal-type sending unit.

Chris added these final details: "I had to weld a bracket on the rear axle to hold a brake line T. Bleeding the brakes necessitates unbolting the front calipers and rotating them back on the rotors so the bleeders face straight up. Jeff Kugel at Kugel

The fuel tank from Tanks, Inc., drops right in place between the rails and bolts to holes already punched in the tops of the rails.

Like most SO-CAL frames, this one uses a Vega-style steering box mounted so the steering shaft comes right through the left-side motor mount.

Komponents made up a steering shaft with some Borgeson U-joints specifically for my application. He also supplied me with some nylon bushings originally meant to fit a Jag-style rear radius arm, so I could use them for steering shaft bearings in the steering column. They had to be cut down for my application though, since I'm going to run a 1 1/2-inch steering column. The steering column will connect to a Vega-style steering gear."

The installed front suspension looks very traditional, right down to the black SO-CAL flexible front brake hoses.

Chris explains that the rest of the project will include a body from Rod Bods "and a Richmond manual transmission from SO-CAL with a long-sliding-rail shifter. As I started buying parts from SO-CAL, they helped out by locating parts at prices better than most mail-order companies, which really helped. SO-CAL also supplied the Lakewood bell housing, which they modified specifically for the chassis and clutch linkage (see chapter 8 for more on the SO-CAL clutch linkage). The 22-pound flywheel, disc, pressure plate, and throw-out bearing are from McLeod. As for the engine, right now it's the 327 in the garage, but if everything goes as planned, I'll be running a Holley-headed and inducted 350."

Epilogue

Between the time these photos of Chris' project were taken, and the publication of the book, Chris assembled the roadster and drove it to a few local events. To quote Pete Chapouris, "We're all very impressed by Chris' eagerness and first-time ability."

The finished frame, ready to be disassembled again so all the pieces can go out for plating, polish, and paint.

Chapter 2

The Frame

Hot rodders tend to spend a large percentage of their money on things they can see, with the most obvious parts of the car often getting the most attention. Who can fault a builder for spending enormous amounts of time and energy blocking out all the body panels and then paying serious money to have a talented painter apply a multistage candy paint job complete with clearcoats and polishing?

Yet, there are times when the best money *should* be spent on things you can't see. Which is more important, the chrome valve covers or the roller-rocker assemblies underneath them? The polished intake manifold or the high-lift cam? The painted finish on the outside of the block or the microfinish on the reground crankshaft journals?

In this chapter we want to be sure each builder gives serious consideration to the biggest component (or series of components) on the car that can't be seen. By that, we mean the one thing that ties the whole thing together: the frame.

Not only does the frame tie the whole car together, it affects the car's style, height, ride, handling, and cost. A pro/street coupe with a 502-cid crate motor will have a very different frame from one that's built as a flathead-powered nostalgia car.

As discussed in chapter 1, most of your frame decisions should be determined during the planning part of the project. A nostalgia car needs a nostalgia frame. Something like the boxed Deuce frame offered by SO-CAL, with buggy springs on both ends and a dropped axle with hairpin radius rods. If you want the car super low, it's far better to determine that in the very beginning than it is to assemble the car and then have to modify the suspension later to get it down in the weeds.

Horsepower always has its cost. Not just the cost of the high-output big-block, or the modified 700 R4 transmission, but the cost of a *chassis strong* enough to handle that power. When you drop the hammer and send 400 foot-pounds of torque to two sticky 12-inch-wide tires, it puts a hell of a load on the entire chassis, from the axle to the leaf springs, to the frame rails and cross-members.

This '32 Ford frame from SO-CAL offers the benefits of a boxed frame while still providing a recessed area along the inside of the frame rail to neatly run brake and fuel lines. The frame can be set up for highboy or full-fendered cars and comes with coil-overs or buggy rear spring. *SO-CAL*

Before starting on the frame you need to know all the basic dimensions for the car: the wheelbase, the distance between the frame and the ground at both the front and rear, and the track width of the front and rear tires. With these dimensions in hand, you can do a sketch of the new frame. Unless your project is really unusual, you will probably want to have a drawing or blueprint of a stock frame as well—one that shows the axle centerlines, the location of important body-mounting holes, and the width of the frame at various points.

Your Options Are . . .

Once you know what you need in a frame, in terms of the wheelbase and other hard dimensions, you're faced with three basic options, each with one or more variations. Essentially, you can work with the original frame, build your own frame from rails, or buy a complete aftermarket frame.

Use That Old Frame

For rodders who bought a complete car, running or not, the option of using the original frame may be attractive. Cost is always a consideration, and using that gennie frame means you don't have to buy a frame from Fat Man or TCI or one of the many manufacturers of new street rod frames. In your mind you may figure that old frame needs only a little cleaning and repair before being recycled back into service. For anyone

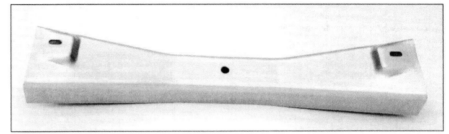

The front cross-member from SO-CAL is designed to both lower the car 1 inch and provide plenty of positive caster. By providing for extra positive caster the cross-member allows cars to run 6 to 9 degrees of net caster, after the car is raked 2 or 3 degrees—all without putting a bind in the front spring. *SO-CAL*

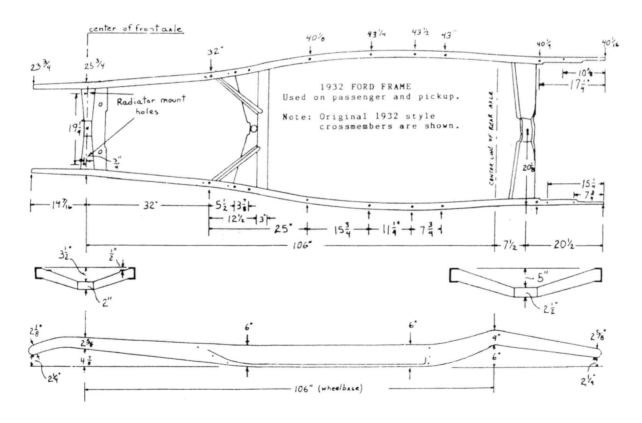

A mechanical drawing like this one for a '32 Ford provides all the basic dimensions for the frame. Street rod vendors and many aftermarket frame manufacturers can often supply a similar drawing for most popular cars.

23

who buys an old Cadillac, Studebaker, or other "unusual" car, using the original rails may be the *only logical* approach.

Yes, you can use a good original frame and many hot rodders do. Experienced builders warn, however, that using an old, substandard frame often works out to be more work and cost more money than the builder originally figured.

An original frame should be inspected, but first you need to get it really clean, which often means hauling it over to a sandblaster. Once it's been blasted clean, you can carefully inspect the frame. Look for stress cracks, serious rust (serious enough to weaken the frame), or evidence of past accidents. With a factory blueprint in hand, you can check the gennie frame against the factory dimensions.

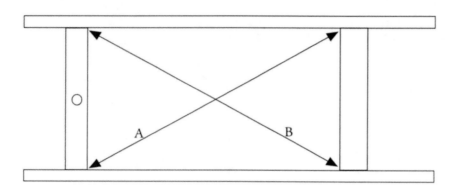

Whether the frame is old or new, it's a good idea to check the measurements from one corner to the other. Starting from known reference points—like the cowl-mounting holes on many Ford frames—you will want to find the axle centerlines. Once you've found those points, or some other quality reference points, make sure that A equals B. It's a good idea to check the X-measurements using more than one set of reference points.

With the frame on jack stands you can do some simple dimensional checks. Perhaps more important is the check made, corner to corner, to ensure the frame isn't out-of-square. When measuring, use the right reference points. At SO-CAL they recommend measuring from the rivet holes in the front and rear cross-members and the cowl-mounting holes. Then, put the frame on three jack stands, one at each rear corner, and one in the middle of the front cross-member or spreader bar. Once you've leveled the rear cross-member, take the level to the front cross-member and see if that one's level as well.

If you're unsure as to whether or not a particular frame is worth saving, haul it down to the local street rod or fabrication shop and get their opinion on the frame's condition and the cost for any needed repairs.

Updating an Original Frame

Your car's original frame probably wasn't intended to handle the power of a 350-ci small-block, but boxing will help reinforce it. Templates can be cut from light cardboard and then used to mark the boxing material. Most experienced frame fabricators recommend using steel plate that's the same thickness as the frame material. You should box at least the central part of the frame rails where the X-member will attach. More prudent would be using boxing plates that run up as far as the engine mounts or even the front cross-member. Pete explains, "We box from the front cross-member back past the firewall, and where all cross-members mount, if full boxing is not desired."

The original X-member (if one was used) will likely have to be reinforced as well, and modified to accept the tail housing of the new transmission. By the time you've opened up the cross-member enough to take a Turbo 400 transmission, it might be easier just to add in an aftermarket cross-member. And by the time you've done that and boxed all or part of the rails, it often turns out to be less money and hassle in the long run just to bite the proverbial bullet and buy a new frame right from the get go.

There isn't anything that can't be repaired, though, and that includes your original frame. It's more a matter of whether or not it makes sense to repair the frame, instead of replacing it with something new. The cost and availability of a new frame are a big part of this equation.

If no one makes a new frame, or a set of rails, for your 1914 Hupmobile, then fixing that old frame might look like a pretty good idea.

Build Your Own

Individuals who want something unusual, who have a knack for fabrication, or who simply insist on doing everything themselves, may opt to start with a set of new rails and work from there. This way you can easily *pinch* the front of the frame rails, or change the axle centerlines slightly so the wheels better fit the fender openings. The cross-members can be as simple or elaborate as you decide you need, crafted by hand or purchased already fabricated from a company like Chassis Engineering or Pete and Jake's, ready to install between your rails. The front suspension can be as simple as a dropped axle, as common as a Mustang

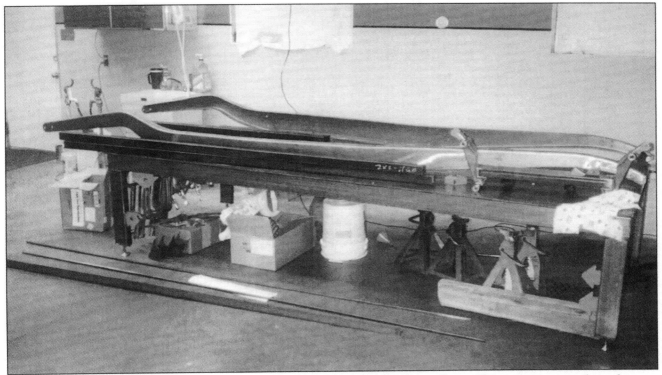

This is the start of the Deuce truck project, a pair of stamped rails from Deuce Frame Company on a sturdy surface table with enough rectangular tubing to make a frame jig or fixture.

II IFS system, or as high-tech as one of the newer independent systems with built-in air bags for instant height adjustment.

Frame rails appear to be a simple piece of mild steel, bent to shape and stamped full of holes for the body and other necessary parts of the car. Like everything else, though, they're not as simple as they seem, and they're certainly not all the same.

Materials

Most of the frames and frame components sold in the street rod industry are made from good old mild steel. Yes, chrome-moly is a more durable material, with greater strength for a given amount of weight, but in most of these applications that extra strength simply isn't needed. SO-CAL uses rails from American Stamping to make their 1932 Ford frames; American Stamping rails are also seen in the how-to sequence in this chapter. Those rails, and 99 percent of the frames seen in catalogs or on display stands at the Nationals, are fabricated from mild steel.

The exceptions to this mild-steel rule are the one-off frames. For instance, each tubular frame rail built by Steve Moal for the Tim Allen Roadster is made from two parallel pieces of chrome-moly tubing. Steve prefers chrome-moly "because of the very high quality of the raw material and because

it's what I'm used to working with." A recently finished Model A truck chassis built at Metal Fab in Minneapolis is another chrome-moly creation. "You don't really need chrome-moly unless it's a high-horsepower application," explains Jim Petrykowski, owner of the Metal Fab shop outside Minneapolis, "or unless it's a real active suspension" (the Model A truck is powered by a blown big-block). Many of the frames that came out of the old Boyd Coddington shop were made entirely or in part from chrome-moly.

Despite Steve Moal's use of round tubing for the RRR Roadster, the typical hot rod frame is made from rectangular rails. The rectangular profile offers good strength, a nice flat surface to mount the body on, and a shape that closely mimics the shape of an original Ford or Chevy frame.

Frame Rails, Stamped or Fabricated

In the case of the 1932 Ford rails from Deuce Frame Company, the rails themselves are stamped from a flat sheet. That way they get a faithful re-creation of the signature Ford frame rail. Most of the other rails seen in the industry are simply made of flat stock, flame or plasma-cut to size and then welded up into a C-channel or a box.

The Deuce Frame Company rails are stamped by an outside company: American Stamping

Here you can see Neal's frame fixture in position on the surface table. This is more elaborate than most builders need, but will make it easier to keep everything in line as the frame is stretched.

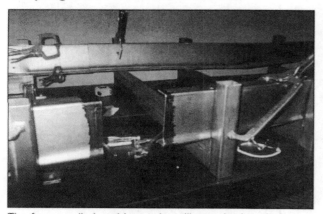

The frame rails in midstretch, still attached to their stations. The area Neal cut is just ahead of the area where the frame kicks up for the rear axle.

The inside of the rails shows the body-mounting nuts in place. It's a good idea to run a tap through these after they are welded in place to clean up the threads.

Group in Olive Branch, Mississippi. Barry Carter, owner of the Stamping Group, describes himself as a tool and die maker. "I've been working in this field since I was 15 years old. In 1977 I made the dies needed to stamp out an automotive bumper; by 1987 they'd made a million bumpers off those same dies."

The same technology is used to make the Deuce frame rails. Barry makes the process sound simple. "The dies are made from hardened steel. Each die is actually made up of various pieces, no one piece is larger than 18 inches long. That way if you do have a problem with a die, you don't have to replace the whole thing. These are all pretty standard manufacturing processes."

With the Deuce rails, there is a die set for the left rail and another for the right. "It takes two hits to form each rail," explains Barry. "The first hit cuts the sheet to size and the second hit actually forms the rail. We use 2,000 tons of pressure to form the rails."

Barry goes on to explain that the difference between good frame rails and not-so-good rails is in the dimensions and the way the rails are formed. "Fabricated rails (fabricated from flat stock) don't have the rounded corners that the originals do. Fabricated rails may also show evidence of grinding on the corners."

No matter which type of rail you buy, be sure the dimensions are correct and that any necessary reference holes or marks are accurate as well. And whether you buy rails or a complete frame, remember that shipping can cause unseen damage. For this reason it's a good idea to carefully check the basic dimensions of rails and frames, and to do some height and cross-measurement checks on a complete frame.

Often the company that manufactures and sells the rails will also sell matching boxing plates. You may even be able to buy the rails longer than stock for a special application. For a look at how one hot rodder assembled a '32 Ford frame from rails, see the In the Shop section later in this chapter.

If building a frame from rails is the answer for your project, you first need a set of engineering drawings for the frame and your own sketch showing where important components like the firewall and radiator shell are located. (Though some of these measurements may change slightly after the first mock-up.)

A wide variety of complete frames are available, including this Model A frame from Pete and Jake's. Advantages include fully boxed rails, already installed cross-members, and body-mounting holes that are already drilled and equipped with 3/8 inch Nut-serts. *Pete and Jake's*

The second thing you need is a good surface table, like the one Neal Letourneau built, shown later in this chapter. The table provides a level work surface that you can bolt or weld frame-rail supports to, and on which you can mark center-lines and dimensions. You can't build a frame that's square and correct in all its dimensions unless you have known and stable references to measure from. All this depends on a good surface table.

If space is tight in your shop, you can design a simplified table with removable legs, so it can be stored against the wall when not in use. But it needs to be sturdy and flat, with an adjustment on each leg to help level the table on the garage floor.

A Brand-New Frame

Buying a brand-new frame offers a number of advantages. First is the "new" part of the description. These frames come without rust, cracks, or old repairs.

The second really nice thing about buying a new frame is the incredible variety of products currently available. Whether you want yours modified in the back for a pro/street application, or with the front suspension already installed, someone likely makes exactly what you have in mind. If you're building a Deuce, you can have anything from a complete nostalgia frame to a high-tech alternative with independent suspension.

Complete frames come as complete as you want. Most manufacturers will sell the frame with or without the front and rear suspension already installed. As mentioned earlier, many frames are available with two or three different types of suspension. You might have your choice of either a dropped front axle with four-bar linkage or a complete independent front suspension with tubular upper and lower control arms and coil-over shocks. Many manufacturers designate their "complete" chassis as Stage I, Stage II, or Stage III, depending on the degree of completeness.

Relatively new on the market are the air-bag suspensions, which provide total ride control. These systems are offered as an option by many of the manufacturers selling complete frame assemblies; they're covered in more detail in the suspension chapters.

Another advantage of the complete frame is the added strength built into the new frame. Many of these come with boxed rails and stout cross-members already in place. You don't have to box or reinforce your old frame, or even add boxing plates to those new stamped rails; everything's been done for you. When deciding whether or not you need boxed rails, consider that many of the original frames used a double U-shaped channel, with *one inside the other*. The smaller, inside rail often angled away from the

Most street rod vendors will supply a complete frame either bare or already equipped as a roller. This 1932 Ford frame comes with either a dropped axle or independent suspension, and a 9-inch Ford housing at the rear. It can also be ordered with stainless AN brake lines already installed. *TCI*

Among the many offerings in the frame category is this complete frame with air-bag suspension already installed. *Art Morrison*

make frames from round tubing instead of channels and rectangular tubing. The double row of tubing used to form the "ladder" side channels makes for a strong frame, though it may be more challenging to drill holes and attach brackets to a round tube. A few of these frames even come in chrome-moly instead of mild steel.

Before buying a brand-new frame, be sure it will match up to the body you intend to use. Some of the aftermarket frames locate the cross-members in such a way that a genuine Ford or Chevy body won't drop into place correctly unless you cut out sections of the floor first. One builder I know had to cut the floor out of a very nice, original Ford body in order to use the new frame he'd already purchased. Most manufacturers don't volunteer this information, you have to ask!

New cross-members and X-members need to be considered with the same criteria in mind. Make sure they'll clear the tail housing on that TH400 or R4 transmission, and that they allow room to run the large-diameter dual exhaust pipes that you intend to install. Again, be certain these parts will work in tandem with your intended body so it will set down into place without any modifications.

main rail to form the X-member. Building such frames is cost-prohibitive today. The boxed rails offer more strength and a good surface for attaching the cross-members or X-members.

For those who like things high-tech, Kugel Komponents, Mike Adams Rod Shop, and a few others

Unusual projects call for unusual chassis. This fully independent chassis is the result of a collaboration between Kugel Komponents and Oldsmobile. The rear-mounted engine is an Aurora powerplant. Note the rocker-arm independent front suspension. *Kugel*

If you like your rear tires really fat, try this pro/street frame from TCI. Available for 1928 to 1941 Fords, it comes either as a bare frame or with front and rear suspension and axles installed. *TCI*

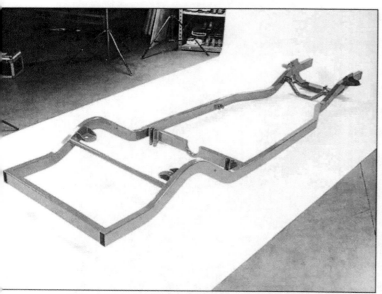

This perimeter frame utilizes mandrel-bent 2x4-inch tubing featuring 0.120-inch wall thickness. These ProFile frames are available to fit many popular cars and can be equipped with air suspension, or any one of a number of conventional suspension systems. *Art Morrison*

Not all hot rodders believe in the low and slow philosophy. This MaxG chassis utilizes Corvette components in front and a modified four-bar in back, all designed to maximize cornering abilities. *Art Morrison*

Remember that your choice of a frame depends on the end use. You have to decide how you're going to use and equip the new hot rod, and then buy a frame that works best for that use and equipment.

What You Need to Know

Based on your sketches, the original engineering drawing, and the information provided by the frame manufacturer, you should know the following: where the stock axle centerlines are located, where your own choice for axle centerlines is going to be located (some of this may be determined during the mock-up stage), and where the engine will be located.

Don't forget that by positioning the engine a little farther back in the chassis you help to even out the nose-heavy weight distribution of a typical hot rod. Sometimes a simple dimple in the firewall for the distributor or a recessed firewall from a company like Bitchin' will push the engine far enough back that you can install a bigger radiator, fan, and fan shroud.

Too many street rods have been built with the engine so far forward that there really isn't room for a good-size fan, shroud, and radiator. A no-hassle car is one that doesn't overheat while you're cruising around on the fairgrounds. These cars benefit from good components installed with care and planning.

The other common mistake is to place the engine too low in the chassis. To run a big, belt-driven fan you need to place the engine high enough in the chassis that the centerline of the water pump is in the center, or just above the center, of the radiator. If nothing else, leave a minimum of 5 inches between the bottom of the oil pan and the ground. As a rule of thumb for the entire project, nothing should hang down any lower than the bottom of the wheel rims when the suspension is fully compressed.

The Mock-Up

Once you have the frame nearly finished, you can build your car "in the rough." For this exercise, you want to start with the frame rails sitting at ride height. The front suspension can be assembled loosely, enough so you can put the wheels and tires on at least one side. You can effectively lock the height of either the front or rear suspension with solid rods installed in place of the shock absorbers. Leave the coil springs out of the car or off the shocks. For leaf springs, just use the main leaf instead of the whole spring pack. Some builders leave the frame on the table, in the jig used to assemble the frame, but that way you can't experiment with the height of the frame and car.

The idea is to partially assemble the car so you can be sure the body mounting locations are correct. You also need to check the location of the engine,

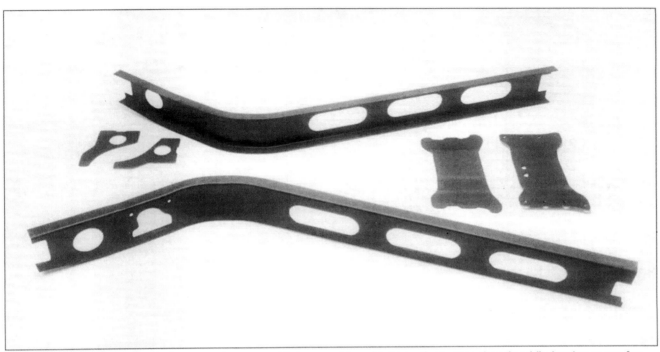

This X-member and transmission mounting assembly is meant to add strength to your chassis while leaving room for most transmissions. *Chassis Engineering*

radiator, and firewall. If you can get the body and running boards mounted temporarily on the car, you can also finalize decisions regarding the rake of the frame and the final position of the rear axle relative to the fender opening. This is also a good time to double check the axle widths, and how they work with your intended wheels and tires.

When assessing the overall look of the car during these mock-up sessions, it's important to be able to get back far enough to really appreciate the car and the proportions. You can't decide how a slight change in the angle of the radiator grille shell will affect the look of the car when your nose is pressed up against the fender.

If the garage is small, you need to be able to roll the car or the whole table outside. At least design the table so it can be turned and positioned so you can open the door and stand outside to check the proportions of all the components. Spend some time looking everything over, take some photos. If a body panel looks out of place in a visual sense, take time to reposition it and then stand back for another look.

If a few body panels are missing, create new ones with cardboard or plywood and tape or

screw them in place. Decide how far back to place the engine and where that puts the firewall. Where, in turn, will that put the driver's feet and the steering column? The builder should avoid thinking that the steering and exhaust will work out later. The position of the steering column must be calculated during the early stages of building. As one experienced builder put it, "Adapt the space to fit the steering, don't adapt the steering to fit the space."

For this exercise, it's handy to have an old engine block and a bare transmission case. You may be able to borrow an old junk engine from a friend, just be sure to put a water pump and fan on the front, and you will need to install a distributor to ensure that it will clear the firewall. The tranny case can often be borrowed as well, or sourced from the parts bin at the local transmission shop.

Everything you do at this stage affects something else. The law of unintended consequences is in full effect here. Don't do this in a hurry. Look for the obvious mistakes you can't see and ask friends for their input before making the final decisions on the location of all the major components.

After the stretch the frame looks like any other Deuce frame, except for the two weld beads on the inside of the left frame rail.

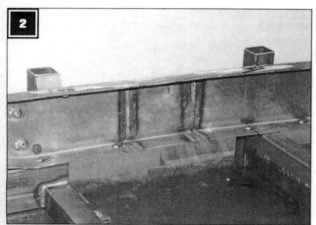

This close-up shows the inside of the rail where the 6-inch section was added and heli-arc welded into place.

*T*he sequence that follows covers the step-by-step construction of the frame that Neal Letourneau built for John Keena's 1932 Ford pickup. Though the frame they're building is modified from stock, there's no reason the same steps couldn't be followed to build a standard wheelbase frame.

Sometimes deciding whether or not to buy a complete frame or build one from scratch is a moot point. When John Keena from Minneapolis decided to build a '32 Ford pickup truck with a stretched cab, he realized that the decision meant an ordinary Deuce frame just wouldn't do the job. John then asked Neal Letourneau of St. Paul, Minnesota, if he could build a '32 Ford frame with a 112-inch wheelbase, instead of Henry's stock measurement of 106 inches.

Neal started with stamped rails from Deuce Frame Company. These rails are actually stamped by American Stamping Company from 11-gauge mild steel and are accurate reproductions of the originals, right down to the signature concave section along the outside of each frame rail. When Neal ordered the frame rails, he also ordered

The inside of the frame rail shows the boxing plate in place. Note that the missing section of the boxing plate does not line up with the stretched part of the frame.

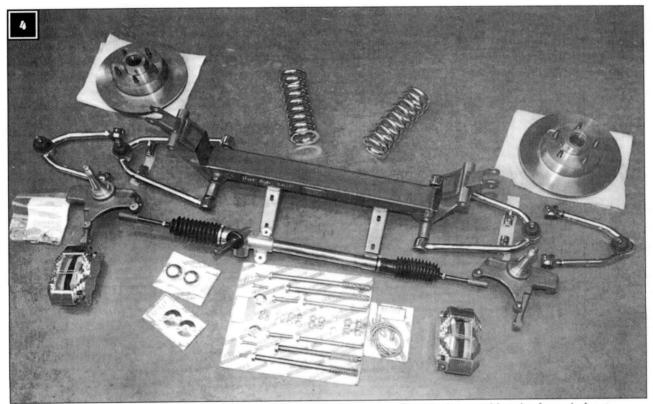

The Heidt's Superide kit provides more than just the front suspension. The kit also provides the frame's front cross-member.

Neal installs the front spreader bar and a piece of rectangular tubing (temporarily) before the front cross-member goes in place. Note the vise-grip and string that mark the frame's centerline.

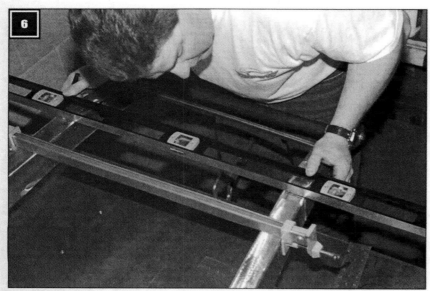

Neal first marks the axle centerline, then makes a second line 1/8 inch ahead of the true centerline. This second line will be the center of the cross-member and is set slightly ahead of the original centerline, because positive caster will push the new axle centerline back slightly.

matching boxing plates from the same company. "Some people only box the frame at the front and the back, where the suspension attaches," says Neal, "but I like to box the whole thing, it adds so much rigidity to the frame. And originally the cross-members were riveted to these frames, but now we weld them in. The boxed frame provides a really substantial structure, something to weld the cross-members to."

The frame is fabricated on the surface table in Neal's shop. This is a simple 4x11-foot table with a surface made up of 1/2-inch steel plate. The whole thing is well supported by a steel framework, with a height adjustment at each leg. "The table is leveled," explains Neal, "and that's the reference for everything to follow."

34

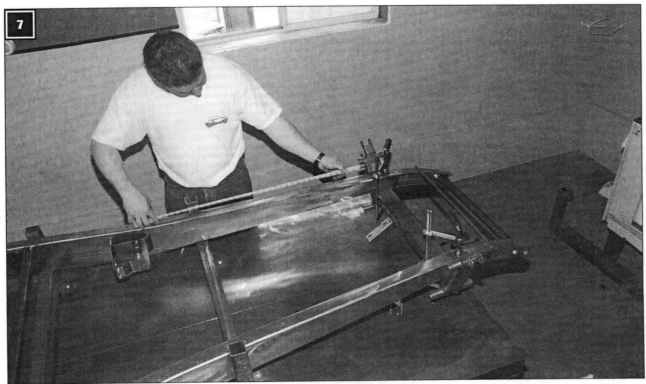

Once the cross-member is clamped in place, Neal can check the position of the brake pedal pivot.

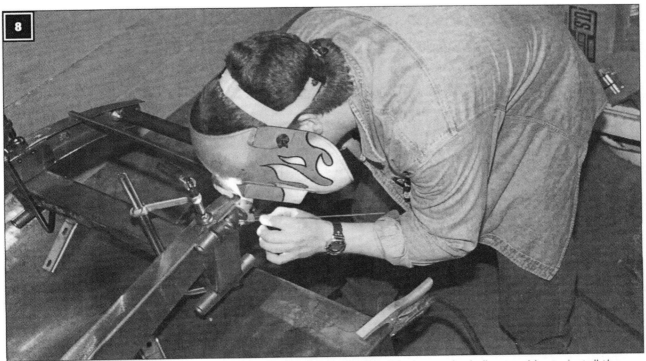

After checking and double-checking the position of the cross-member, Neal uses the heli-arc welder to install the cross-member.

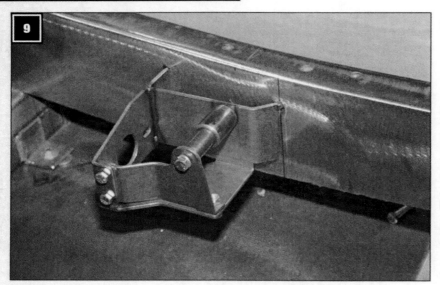

Neal installed the brake pedal pivot and master cylinder support in the recommended position. It's a good idea, however, to tack-weld the bracket in place until the first mock-up is finished. Changes in engine or firewall location can affect the location of the brake pedal.

The mock-up allows Neal (on the right) and John a chance to see how all the pieces fit together to create a whole car. One of the things they need to determine at this stage is whether the "big 'n little" tires (285/70x15 rear and 215/60x14 front) work to give the truck the look they're after.

Neal decided to build the frame, minus cross-members, and then lengthen the frame. As he explains the process: "We started with an engineering drawing of a stock Ford frame that we got from Little Dearborn in St. Paul, but some of the street rod catalogs, like the one from Wescott's, have them too. The drawing has all the dimensions of the stock 1932 Ford frame. I laid everything out on the big table, the centerline and all the dimensions. "Then I built six stations to hold the rails. Each one of these stations bolts into holes that I drilled and tapped into the surface plate. When both the rails were in the right position, I welded the rails to the stations."

Note: Many builders use simple vertical stands to support the frame rails, and spreader bars at the front and rear to establish the initial distance between the rails. In these cases it's important to measure, and possibly adjust, the width of the frame through the center before installing cross-members. Neal built his supports with enough heft, precision, and overkill that he only had to clamp the rails in the cradles and do a few checks of the width before he could tack-weld the rails to the supports.

When Neal bought the rails, he had the foresight to buy an extra section of raw frame rail. As he explains, "You can only stretch the frame near the back, just ahead of where the kick starts up for the rear axle, just before the spot where the body line dies out. To lengthen the frame, all I had to do was cut each rail, then unbolt the stations and move each one forward *exactly* 6 inches and screw it into new holes I'd already drilled in the table."

Neal's description makes more sense after you realize that what he calls "stations" are very substantial cradles, tied together side to side. Because they're so substantial, the rails couldn't twist or change dimension diagonally when the frame was cut into two pieces.

The extra rail material was then cut and trimmed to exactly fit the void in the center, and then welded in place with the heli-arc welder. Once the rails were lengthened Neal could cut each boxing plate into two pieces, weld it into place, and then add the missing 6-inch section.

Grade-8 flange nuts are added inside the frame for all the appropriate body-mounting holes before the boxing plates go on. As the name suggests, the built-in flange on each nut makes it easy to weld these to the rails without damaging the nut itself or the threads (though it's still a good idea to chase the threads with a tap before assembly).

The three central cross-members are fabricated from seamless DOM (drawn over mandrel) mild steel tubing, 1 5/8-inch diameter with 0.125-inch walls. Neal explains that each one has a job: "The front cross-member will hold the back of the transmission, while the center one gives us someplace to mount the exhaust hangers. And the rear one provides the mount for the four-bar brackets. Once I've got them in place I can add flanges to the front one so the tranny can be dropped out later." The complete cross-member won't be finished until after Neal and John have done the first mock-up and know exactly where the engine and transmission mount.

Better Tubes for Better Frames

Terms like *DOM mild steel tubing* require us to back up for a short primer on the various grades of tubing manufactured from mild steel or chromemoly. For help in this department we have the input of Jim Petrykowski, owner of Metal Fab in Blaine, Minnesota. Jim spends most of his days building street rod or race car components, and can often be found at the local airport, working on vintage aircraft. Jim explains that you have to begin the discussion with an understanding of mild steel tubing.

"What we call mild steel is available in a wide variety of shapes and forms," says Jim. "The lowest grade of steel is E.R. Buttweld. This stuff looks like exhaust tubing, the grain is random because it is essentially cold rolled sheet steel cut into strips, rolled up, and welded (the *E.R.* stands for electric-resistance, as in arc welding). It's inexpensive and readily available. This tubing is moderately strong, but the seam is a problem. If you form or bend it, the seam will break at the weld, and it's not uniform in size.

"What's called DOM is made by taking larger-diameter tubing with a welded seam, and drawing it over a die set. Usually you're 'necking down' the tubing to a somewhat smaller size by

During the mock-up it's important to check that the engine is positioned correctly relative to the firewall and the radiator.

Neal and John want a big, belt-driven fan, and realize at this point that there isn't quite enough clearance between the fan and the radiator. The motor will be moved back 1 inch from the position seen here.

For the purpose of the mock-up, the rear fenders are clamped to the frame while the Ford rear end sits on stands.

Like most quality hot rod components, the Superide comes with thorough instructions. Per the instructions Neal measures back a set amount from the reference point, the second spreader-bar hole in this case. Then it's really just a matter of making sure the cross-member is located evenly side to side, that it's square to the centerline, and that it's in exactly the spot the instructions call for.

"The instructions direct you to measure from the second spreader-bar hole to the cross-member," explains Neal, "and I did that, making sure the distance was the same from one side to the other. And even though the frame is in the jig and I know everything is straight, I went ahead and did my cross-measurements, to be absolutely sure the cross-member is positioned correctly before doing the first tack welds."

The position of the cross-member also affects the caster angle, and it's possible to get the cross-member positioned in such a way that it's difficult to obtain the right caster through the available adjustment. Neal explains that he doesn't check the caster of the front end before doing the final welding: "I'm confident that Heidt's has the caster built into the cross-member. Someone working at home for the first time, however, might want to tack the cross-member in, assemble the suspension, and then check the caster before doing the final welding."

drawing it through the die with a bullet-shaped tool in the center.

"By drawing the tubing through the tooling the size becomes more uniform, the wall thickness increases, and the strength of the material is increased. The weakness of the weld is minimized and the tubing can now be more easily formed and bent. Basically the steel companies take rather weak raw tubing and make it much stronger.

"Top-of-the-line tubing is seamless. The easiest way to form seamless tubing is by taking red-hot solid bar stock, piercing it, and then pulling it through a mandrel. The *very* highest quality tubing is cold-drawn seamless, in which case a billet of bar stock is pierced and drawn through dies while it's cold, with lubrication. This process gets the material's grain going in one direction, which makes it easier to bend and form."

Back to the Deuce

The front suspension for this car will be a Superide from Heidt's. Finding an independent suspension to put in a Deuce can be more difficult than some other cars. With a typical Mustang II type of suspension, the spring tower welds to the top of the frame, but on a 1932 Ford the fender is right there and it will run into the spring tower. The Superide is not a Mustang system and does not use spring towers. This system is designed to provide the advantages of independent suspension while fitting neatly under the fenders of a '32 Ford.

The Mock-Up

The next big step is to take the frame out of the cradles so the first mock-up can be done. Neal uses a small support to hold up the front of the frame, and two vertical stands, with spacers, to hold up the back of the frame. Once the frame is set on the table, the big-block engine and transmission is set between the rails in the spot where they think it will eventually sit.

With the frame stationary, Neal and John clamp the cab, radiator *shell*, and hood in place, along with one rear fender. "We wanted primarily to find out where the motor is going to go," explains Neal. "I like a belt-driven fan, so we wanted to see how big a fan we could run and still clear the radiator. A shroud really helps the fan pull air across the radiator, so we are planning to build a custom shroud as well."

14

With the engine sitting in place and the body clamped to the frame, a wooden dowel takes the place of the steering shaft so Neal can check for clearance problems between the shaft and the motor mount.

One of the unanswered questions for Neal and John is the amount of rake that the truck should have. By using simple spacers between the top of the Lincoln Versailles rear end housing and the frame (check the photos to eliminate confusion), Neal and John can easily change the height at the back of the frame and thus the rake. "The height at the front with this Heidt's kit is pretty much set by the suspension, though you can use stock or dropped spindles. We discussed this with Heidt's. We told them what we were building and where we wanted the front end to sit," explains Neal, "and they recommended that we use the dropped spindles that are an option for this suspension kit.

"We know the distance between the bottom of the frame rail, under the cowl area, and the ground, based on other '32s we've looked at. And the vertical location of the rear end housing is set by the rear tire diameter. The thing we don't know at this point is how much rake will look good on this truck."

This first mock-up will also help Neal determine how much the rear end will have to be narrowed. Though it is one of the relatively narrow 9-inch assemblies from a Lincoln Versailles, this rear end still appears to be too wide for the Deuce truck. The wheels (and their offset) used for the mock-up are probably not the final choice. The tires seen here, however, are the actual tires that will be used on this truck, so the height of the rear end during the mock-up is the same as it will be for the finished project. "When you find a combination that works, you need to make whatever changes to the body or chassis are needed to use that combination," explains Neal. "The wheels and tires can really make the car."

During the mock-up, Neal comments, "As many things as we are changing, it's a good idea to have a look now, early on, at how everything fits."

Though the cab is due to be stretched, the dimensions from the cowl forward are the same as stock. One of the goals of this first mock-up is to determine how far back they can push the motor. As Neal explains, "The more you push the motor toward the rear, the more room you take from the inside of the cab, especially the area where the driver and passenger put their feet."

Another item that could be affected by the location of the engine and the firewall is the brake pedal pivot and master cylinder support. The brake pedal mount is from Deuce Factory. The master cylinder is a later-model Corvette manual dual-disc assembly. The pedal mount is designed for the Corvette unit, often used in situations like this. With rather substantial brakes at both ends, John doesn't figure he needs a power booster. For the mock-up, the pedal support is tack-welded to the left-side frame rail at the location recommended by Deuce Factory.

In addition to the firewall, Neal and John begin to make plans for the steering column and shaft. "We bought some 3/4-inch wooden dowel which we can use to do a mock-up shaft more easily than using steel shafts or tubing," explains Neal.

When we leave Neal and John at the end of the first mock-up, they've determined quite a bit about their work-in-progress. They know that if they move the engine back almost 1 inch from the mock-up position, there will still be room for John's feet while providing room for a nice big fan. They also know the rear end needs to be narrowed, and that the frame rail needs to be "C-ed" to provide enough clearance between the top of the rear end housing and the frame. They've begun to work out the position of the steering column and shaft, and the likely routing for the headers.

The next step is to take off the body and remove the engine, then flip the frame over to install the rest of the central cross-member.

In The Shop: *Fabrication of a SO-CAL Frame*

At this point the frame rails have been cleaned up and mounted in Todd's rather substantial frame jig. Tom has already begun the task of fitting the boxing plates to the right-side frame rail.

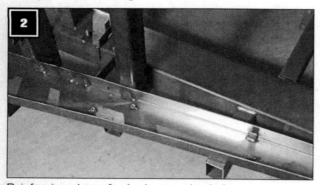

Reinforcing plates for body-mounting holes are positioned so they hold the boxing plates just inside the lip of the frame rail. Additional small "stands" are used wherever necessary to help support the boxing plate.

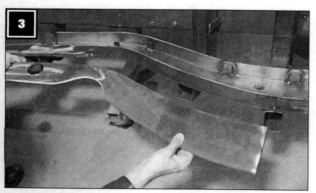

Three separate pieces make up the boxing plate for each side. Each one must be test fit before being welded to another one.

When Pete Chapouris set out to build a new Deuce frame, he didn't want to simply add one more to the long list of aftermarket hot rod frames currently available. What Pete wanted was a unique, high quality frame developed specifically for the 1932 Ford. Having built plenty of frames himself, Pete had a list of features he wanted incorporated into his frame.

The biggest thing that separates the SO-CAL frame from so many others is the unique Step-Boxed™ design. Many frames offer "boxed" rails as a way of increasing the strength of the rail. But in order to make these frames as neat as possible, the bead is ground away after the welding is finished. Now this might make for a nice neat frame rail, but by grinding off the visible bead you also grind off much of the metal that holds the boxing plate to the rail.

The other little problem with a typical boxed rail is the way the brake and fuel lines, electrical cables, and anything else that's clamped to the inside of the rail, are left out in the open. Yes, you can put some of that plumbing inside the rail, but that introduces a whole new set of problems. Pete's idea was to create a new style of frame rail that would provide more strength than the typical boxed frame without any of the disadvantages.

Thus was born the SO-CAL Step-Boxed frame. By recessing the boxing plates slightly from the edge of the rail, there is no need to grind the weld. The resulting rail benefits from the strength of an unground fillet weld. And by recessing the boxing plates slightly, the brake and fuel lines can be tucked neatly up into the corner where they're out of the way and protected by the edge of the rail.

The SO-CAL frame also incorporates its own front cross-member, one designed to keep the front end low while providing plenty of caster for the front axle, even with the car on a three or four degree rake. The SO-CAL Step-Boxed frame is both strong and light. It's a unique frame designed to provide the enthusiast with a good foundation for a unique hot rod.

In order to show exactly what a SO-CAL frame is made of, we've decided to follow the construction of a frame from start to finish. In order to keep

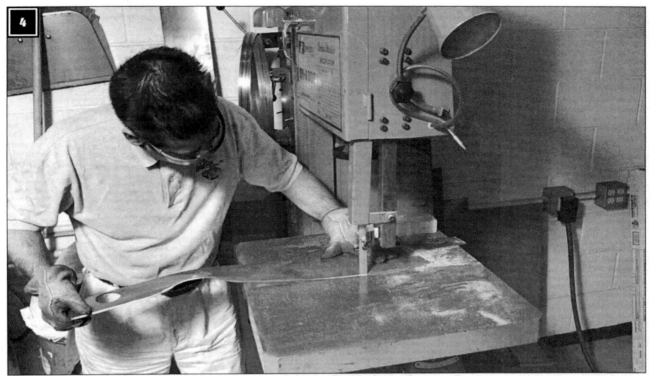

Tom trims the rearmost section of boxing plate so it better fits inside the frame rails.

Each piece of the boxing plate is set in place and fit, then the three pieces are welded into one before being set back into the frame for the last time.

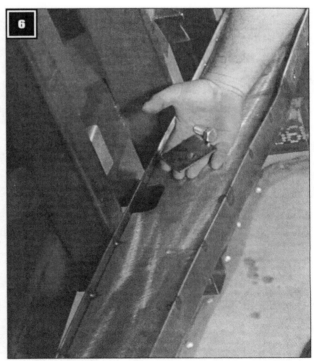

A small bracket, bolted into the cowl-mounting hole, matches the cutout in the boxing plate and ensures that the boxing plate is in exactly the right position.

A ruler or tape is used to ensure the tack welds will be perfectly spaced 4 inches apart. Final welding will be done one 4-inch section at a time. Tom or Todd will do one section, then move across or down the rail to reduce warpage.

At this point it's time to add the cross-members and mounting points for things like the steering gear.

This jig, used here to mark the area that must be cut out so the axle can be set lower in the frame, is another part of Todd's modular fixture. Once the area is marked, Tom will cut the notch in the frame rail with a cut-off wheel.

their shop focused on car building, Pete has arranged to have the frames fabricated at a nearby shop. The shop is owned by Todd Walton, long-time welder, fabricator and hot rod enthusiast.

How it's Done

Construction of a complete SO-CAL frame starts with a set of bare, stamped frame rails. Based on his lengthy experience at another big chassis shop, Todd constructed a very sturdy frame fixture. The fixture, mounted on a rotisserie to make fabrication as easy as possible, ensures that each frame constructed for SO-CAL is both accurate and has exactly the same dimensions as every other frame.

By working closely with SO-CAL, Todd's been able to fine tune the fixture to create frames with a very high degree of accuracy—what you might call built-in repeatability. A good example is in the back of the frame. As Todd explains it, "When we pull the frame out of the jig, the rails spring in a little bit, due to the stresses of welding-in the boxing plate. We noticed that right away and modified the jig slightly. Now, when the rails spring in, they spring in to exactly the right dimension."

Part of the work of building a frame includes preparing the rails before construction. "The rails need a little work when we get them," says Todd. "My main welder, Tom Blair, takes the time to trim away the minor wavy areas on the top or bottom of the rail, before we start construction."

Once the rails are prepped, they can be mounted in the frame jig. "We locate the rails using the cowl-mounting hole, already punched in the rails, as our reference," explains Todd. "Each rail is clamped to the side supports and then tack-welded in place. If you just clamp them in place there's always the chance they might shift during fabrication."

With the rails in the fixture, the next job is to install the backup plates for the body mounting holes and the little "stands" used to help position the stepped boxing plates that are unique to the SO-CAL chassis. Todd explains that the body mounting holes are already stamped in the top of the frame rails by the manufacturer, "But we put the plates in behind the hole, and later those will be drilled and tapped for the body mounting bolts." The little "backup" plates are cut and positioned so they also function as spacers to position the boxing plate just inside the edge of the rails (check the photos here to eliminate confusion). Todd and Tom put the small stands in anywhere there aren't enough backup plates to hold the boxing plate in place.

Todd has the boxing plates laser cut out locally, from mild steel of the same gauge as the railss. Though the cutting is quite accurate they often need a little grinding and finishing to fit just perfect inside the rails. Todd tried having the boxing plates cut out in one piece, but they were just too long and unwieldy. The current program is to cut them in three separate pieces for each frame rail. After Tom has the spacers and small stands in place inside the rails, each of the three pieces is trimmed as necessary and then set into the frame.

Tom tack welds the three pieces into one, then pulls the new one-piece boxing plate out of the frame and carefully welds each of the seams be-

Once the cutout area is finished, Tom can fit the SO-CAL cross-member to the frame. Small fabricated "buttons" between the cross-member and the frame jig help to correctly position the cross-member.

Among the sub-assemblies that are part of the fixture are these designed to aid in the creation of the motor mounts.

tween the plates. Before the final installation of the boxing plate Tom grinds the welded seams until they disappear. To position the boxing plates with precision inside the frame rails, Tom has fabricated a small locating spacer that's held in place with a bolt through the cowl-mounting hole.

The boxing plates are clamped in place with a series of Vise Grips, then Tom marks the seam every four inches with a ruler. The marks help

The finished motor mount snaps in to part of the frame fixture before being welded in place.

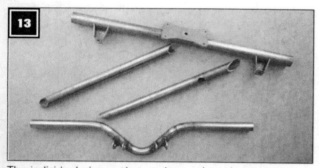

The individual pieces that make up the tubular cross-members are cut and bent at another outside shop before being welded to the frame.

Near the end of the project, Tom pieces together the main central cross-member and the fixtures needed to hold it in the right position.

Tom keep the tack welds neatly spaced. When it comes time for final-welding, Tom and Todd will only do one four inch section at a time before moving down or across the rail to another four inch section. In that way they avoid concentrating too much heat in one part of the rail.

Next comes creation of the notch at the front of the frame that allows these cars to run in the weeds. Tom starts by spraying the area at the front of the rails with Dykem. Then the area to be notched is marked on the frame rails based on the outline of a special template. Following the outline Tom uses a die grinder and cut-off wheel to notch the rail. Small squares of mild steel are cut and tack-welded into the notched area. Then the small plates, and the front ten or so inches of the boxing plate, are final-welded, and finished with a nifty little mini belt sander.

Cars with dropped axles must have the front cross-member positioned correctly or it can be hard to get the correct caster setting without putting a bind in the spring. The SO-CAL front cross-member is specially shaped to allow for plenty of caster. Yet it must still be positioned correctly or all the extra engineering that went into the cross-member will count for nothing. Tom carefully sets the cross-member in place, which requires trimming some metal off the ends. The idea of course is to get the cross-member centered between the rails, which requires some careful trimming, checking and trimming again before he can tack-weld, and then final-weld the cross-member in place.

Todd's frame fixture is a modular affair, and includes subassemblies that Tom uses to correctly locate things like the motor mounts and the central cross-member. At this point Tom uses the fixture to check the position of the motor mounts and to weld in the upper bung needed to locate the Vega-style steering gear. A stock SO-CAL frame mounts the gear below the left

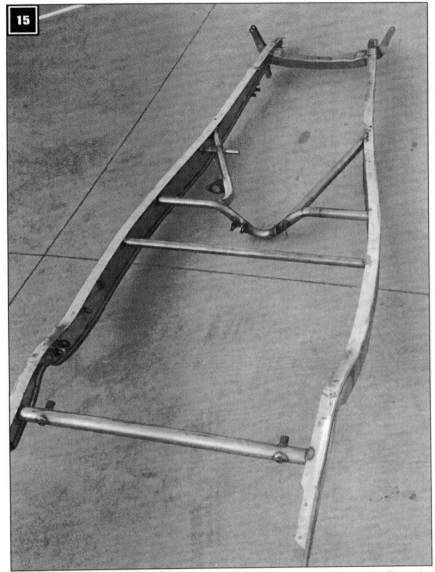

Not the same frame, but a slightly different, finished, SO-CAL frame. Though they look simple, a lot of careful planning and attention to detail go into each one of these chassis.

side motor mount, the mounts themselves are welded up in a separate small jig.

The central cross-member, which in this case could be called a "K-member" by its shape, is made up of a series of pre-cut tubes, made from .120-inch wall thickness mild steel tubing. With the help of the fixture and a whole raft of clamps, Tom sets the tubing in place and then begins to tack-weld the tubing and rear motor mounts in place.

The tubing used to make the various cross-members is designed to slide into a matching hole pre-cut in the boxing plate. "This way, there are no gaps to fill," explains Todd. "If you butt-weld the cross-members there's always some gaps that have to be filled. With no gaps to fill there's no tendency for the frame to 'draw' to the wrong dimension after it comes out of the jig."

With the cross-members in place Tom and Todd can carefully work their way across all the seams with the heli-arc welder. The final welding is spread out over the frame and over time, to limit the amount of heat put into the frame and thus minimize any warpage.

Before being shipped to SO-CAL the frame is carefully finished. Tom details the whole frame, so that when it leaves the shop it's basically "polished" and ready for paint.

Chapter 3

Front Suspension

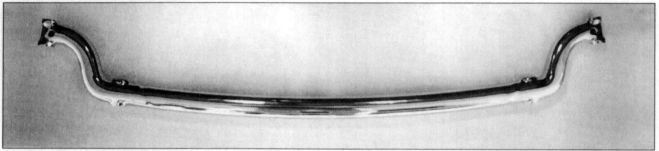

This 4-inch dropped tube axle is available in various widths, with either a 2- or 2 1/4-inch perch boss. Chrome plating is available as well. *Super Bell*

The overall style of the car will be the biggest factor dictating which front suspension is right for you. There's no point in spending the extra money for a polished independent suspension if the car is a resto-rod or very traditional ride.

As Pete Chapouris likes to say, "If it's an open-wheeled car, then it needs a dropped axle. If it's a fat car, then we *might* want to put an independent front suspension under it."

In addition to the car's style, the usage and your personal opinion are important factors when trying to decide which of the many available front suspensions to install. If you want to go around corners like a Ferrari, a dropped axle won't do the job. Ask yourself, "How do I like to drive? What do I expect from this car in terms of handling and cornering?"

Remember that the front suspension is very important for at least three reasons: it's generally more visible, it carries more weight, and it steers the car. Choosing the front suspension is one of the more complex decisions you'll need to make while planning and building the car. This is a situation where each menu choice leads to another menu. Choose a dropped axle for example, and the next menu asks whether you want to use four-bar linkage or split wishbones to hold the axle in place. Click on the four-bar option, and the next drop-down window asks whether you want to use a tubular or I-beam type of axle.

Kingpin kits include the pins themselves, the bushings that need to be pressed into the spindle and then reamed to fit, the bearings that support the spindle, and assorted hardware. *Deuce Factory*

Which Suspension Is Right?

In theory an independent front suspension handles and rides better than a dropped axle. With a twin A-arm suspension system installed under your car, a bump encountered by one wheel has less impact on the other wheel and the occupants of the car. As the name implies, by

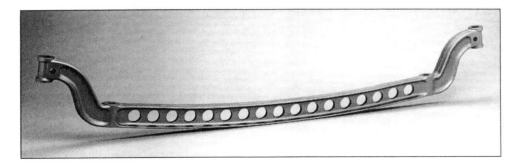

The traditional look calls for a dropped front axle. This drilled axle is made from forged steel and comes in a 47 1/2-inch width. *SO-CAL*

acting independently each wheel is better able to rise up over bumps and steer around corners while keeping a good grip on the road.

I-Beam Axles

There is, however, nothing much cooler than a nice dropped axle mounted with a buggy spring up front and a pair of split radius rods to hold it all in place. So, as Pete Chapouris points out, the choice of a front axle (especially on an open-wheeled car) is largely an aesthetic decision.

Having made that decision, the next choice is the type of linkage you're going to use to hold the axle in place. The nostalgia craze seems to get stronger and stronger, which means that more and more hot rodders are choosing the very traditional split wishbones or hairpin radius rods. The other option is a four-bar linkage—what might be called the choice of a modern traditionalist.

Purists will point out the fact that hairpin radius rods (or split wishbones) put a slight twist on the axle when only one wheel goes over a bump. The twist occurs because each axle end has its own pivot

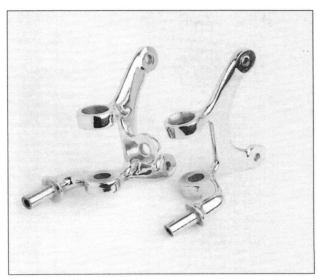

For traditional cars there's nothing like a pair of hairpin radius rods with stainless steel batwings. These batwings come with a provision for mounting the Panhard rod. *SO-CAL*

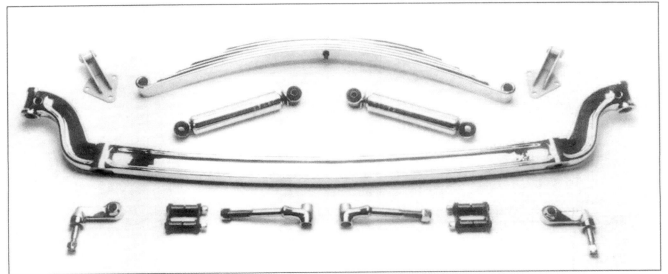

Buying the front axle and suspension as a kit offers a number of advantages: you know everything fits, and that all the components are designed to work together. This EasyRider kit comes with a 47-inch forged, *dropped axle, a matching* spring, adjustable shocks, and all necessary hardware. *Chassis Engineering*

point. Essentially the wheel that hits the bump swings upward on the arc of the radius rod, so it experiences a caster change while the other does not. Replacing radius rods with a four-bar linkage solves that problem. Because the four-bar linkage acts as a parallelogram, one or both ends of the axle can go up or down with no caster change and no twist on the axle. (Be sure to read Pete's sidebar in this chapter and to check the illustrations.)

The twist that an early-Ford axle experiences while going over a bump is the reason you can't use a tubular dropped axle with split wishbones.

Modern tubular axles consist of a center tube with cast or forged ends welded to it. Tubular structures resist twisting, so the twist will cause the welds to fail, if not today, then next week.

Many of these decisions and their implications are made easier by manufacturers who offer their suspension systems as a kit. Buy the axle and the linkage comes along as part of the package. Many go so far as to make the spring, spring perches, spindles, and brakes all part of the assembly you buy.

If you prefer to buy components individually,

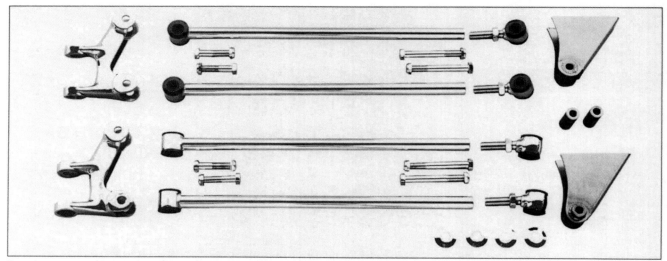

Four-bars became popular with the advent of the dropped tube axle, though some people like them simply for their visual appeal. This kit uses all stainless components and urethane bushings. *Deuce Factory*

CASTER

Having the correct caster for your car means it will go down the highway in a straight line without the need for constant minor steering corrections. Caster also helps the steering wheel return to the straight-ahead position after a turn. The caster recommendations are very different between straight axles and independent suspension, with most straight axles needing considerably more positive caster. *SO-CAL*

Most builders recommend the use of a Panhard rod when a dropped axle is installed with cross-steer linkage, as seen in this demonstration Deuce frame. *TCI*

Camber is simply the tilt of the tire in or out as seen from the font. True vertical is zero camber, a tilt to the outside at the top is positive, a tilt to the inside is negative. *SO-CAL*

you need to be sure all the pieces will work together on your particular frame. Already mentioned is the need to avoid using split wishbones with a tube axle. Another common mistake is the use of heim joints or spherical rod ends at the end of a four-bar link. As Eric Aurand from Chassis Engineering explains, "You only want four-bars to move in one plane vertically, but spherical rod ends allow lateral movement. That lateral movement gives the car what I call a 'beer truck' kind of ride." What should be used there instead are the simple urethane bushings that come with most four-bar kits.

Most dropped axles are available in two or three widths. Unlike a rear axle assembly that is measured flange to flange, front axle widths are measured between kingpin centerlines. The drilled and dropped axle in the SO-CAL catalog comes in a 47 1/2-inch width. The common 46- and 48-inch width became standardized in typical hot rod fashion. As Jim Petrykoski from Metal Fab explains: "The original Ford axles were something like 50 or 52 inches wide, but when people started to *drop* the axle, they just reshaped it, which meant it got narrower. When Jim Ewing started Super Bell Axle Company, he offered a dropped axle in a 48-inch width. Then when the first disc brakes were offered, they moved *the wheel* out about an inch on either side, so pretty soon Jim offered a 46-inch axle for cars with disc brakes. In the end, what you're trying to do is put a 5 1/2- or 6-inch wheel, 14 or 15 inches in diameter, on a stock car with fenders and still be able to use the full turn radius."

When working with dropped axles, you also need to consider the distance between the bosses for the spring perches. That measurement must match the length of the spring you intend to use. The front cross-member used on early-Ford frames is another piece that must be chosen to match all the

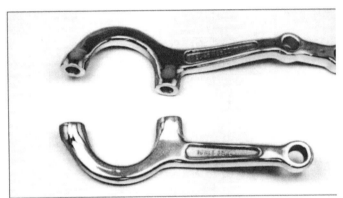

Steering arms come in a variety of shapes and need to be matched up with the spindle and the axle support linkage. You have to be sure the steering linkage clears the four-bars or split wishbones. *Super Bell*

others. Early hot rodders discovered years ago that the use of a Model A front cross-member in a Deuce frame would lower the front of the car. Today, SO-CAL makes a cross-member designed for use in both Model A and 1932 frames that lowers the front end by 1 inch.

A discussion of the front cross-member brings up the subject of caster. (See the illustrations in this chapter for a refresher course in front-end alignment terms.) Most hot rodders want their car to have some rake, with the front end lower than the rear. It gives the car that aggressive stance and a sense of motion—almost like they're moving when they're standing still. That's all fine and good, but as you raise the back and lower the front, you tip the front axle forward and lose some of your caster angle. So you need to buy a cross-member with a little extra caster built in, or install the cross-member with a little extra angle.

For extra sex appeal, try this pushrod independent front suspension. It must be used with an extended frame, so there is room for the coil-overs behind the radiator. *Kugel Komponents*

As Pete Chapouris explains, "People forget that when you rake the car, the caster goes negative. You might need 9 degrees of caster to net out at 6. Our cross-member allows you to run more positive caster without putting a bind in the spring or the spring shackle."

Some controversy surrounds the use of a Panhard rod with a buggy-spring dropped-axle front suspension. A Panhard rod attaches to the axle on one side of the car, and to the frame on the other, and minimizes side-to-side motion between the axle and frame. Though there are plenty of hot rods out there with straight axles and no Panhard rod, Pete Chapouris feels the Panhard rod is a necessary part

of a straight axle installation. "Basically, if you use a buggy spring and a cross-steer setup, then you need a Panhard rod. Without a Panhard rod, with a Vega cross-steer, you cause the axle to swing on the shackles, creating 'bump steer.' We also like to install a steering damper; it ensures there is no side-to-side shimmy. Our straight-axle installations always include a Panhard rod and damper."

Preventing Bump Steer

We've all heard the term "bump steer," meaning that a bump will cause the car to move from the steering line chosen by the driver. These little problems crop up when the axle and the steering

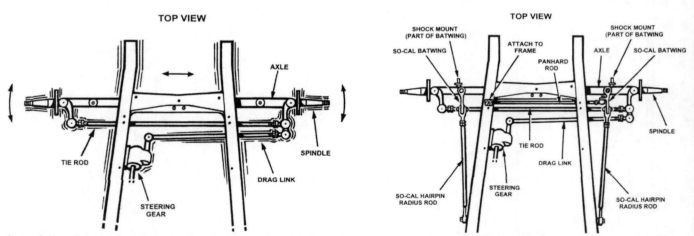

A straight axle, with buggy spring or transverse springs, can move relative to the frame unless a Panhard rod is used. For this reason SO-CAL recommends the use of a Panhard rod, and has designed a bracket for the Panhard rod into the right-side batwing. It's important to note that unless it is properly laid out and installed, a Panhard rod can cause as many problems as it solves. *SO-CAL*

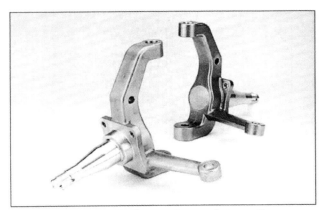

Among the many spindles on the market are these examples, which are investment cast from 17-4 stainless steel. These spindles will accept a wide variety of disc brake options. *Art Morrison*

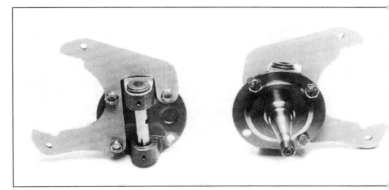

These forged spindles are available to fit a variety of axles, and come with or without the kingpins already fitted. The spindle is also available with a "GM snout" and the correct brackets so the disc brake rotor and caliper slide right into place. *Chassis Engineering*

linkage move through different arcs as the car goes over a bump.

Though problems can occur with any type of steering, the bump-steer problem is best illustrated by looking at drag link steering. Bump steer in this system occurs when the bump causes the axle to move forward or back more than the drag link as they swing through their arcs. The effect is a little different depending on the style of axle mounting, but the end result is the same. Basically, the axle and the end of the drag link that attaches to the axle must move through the same arcs as the suspension moves up-and-down over bumps.

In a cross-steer application, such as with a Vega or Saginaw steering box, bump steer is caused by side-to-side axle movement, rather than front-to-rear. Any axle movement to the side during suspension travel will push or pull on the drag link, causing the dreaded bump-steer problem. As mentioned by Pete Chapouris, street rods with a transverse leaf spring mounted with a shackle at either end can allow lateral axle movement on the shackles. To avoid this problem, most street rod equipment manufacturers recommend a Panhard rod. The Panhard rod prevents side-to-side axle movement, but it must be designed and mounted very carefully so as not to create more problems than it solves.

General installation guidelines include the need to keep the Panhard rod parallel to, and the same length as, the drag link. More specific recommendations can be had by consulting with the manufacturer of the front suspension and linkage. With these cross-steer applications, the steering gear and linkage should be mounted so the pitman arm is pointing straight ahead when the gear is in the center of its movement. It is also important that the gear be mounted so the drag link is parallel to the tie rod.

Another cause of front-end shimmy is worn

These Mustang spindles are available either stock height or dropped. Both are made of steel instead of cast iron. *Heidt's*

kingpins or axle ends. With loose or worn kingpins and bushings, a bump in the road can induce the dreaded "straight axle shimmy." When installing a dropped axle, you have to be sure the pins fit tight in the ends of the axle (sometimes a problem with used axles) and that the bushings in the spindle are correctly reamed for a good fit between the bushing and the pin. Many hot rod suppliers will ream the bushings before the axle or spindles are shipped. It's one of those jobs that requires precision and should be done by an experienced shop. If you buy spindles and need to have the bushings installed and/or reamed, any good shop that services trucks or truck chassis should be able to help you out. The other thing to keep in mind after the dropped axle is installed is the need for frequent applications of lubrication. Though we've all become accustomed to no-lube tie rod ends and ball joints, kingpin bushings still require frequent attention from that old-fashioned grease gun hanging on the wall.

Independent Front Suspension Designs

Independent front suspension systems come in a wide variety of styles and prices. For the budget-minded rodder, a number of companies offer a Mustang II-type front suspension cross-member. You install the cross-member in your new or old frame and then add the suspension components, either stock Mustang or aftermarket. These can be scrounged at the local used parts emporium or purchased new. Most street rod companies in this market offer various upgrades over the stock Ford pieces.

The first upgrade usually replaces the narrow lower arm and its support strut with a much wider lower arm that doesn't need the strut. This makes for a cleaner installation and eliminates the strut support. Most companies also offer tubular upper and lower arms to replace the original stamped steel arms. Of course you can go one step further and order the arms in chrome or polished stainless for extra glitter.

If you are looking for more than a simple Mustang II suspension, a number of companies build complete stand-alone front suspension systems that come with the cross-member, the arms, spindles, and all necessary hardware. Some of these assemblies have been designed from scratch

These chrome-plated coil-overs are available for Mustang suspensions and offer the advantage of adjustable ride height and extra sparkle. *Heidt's*

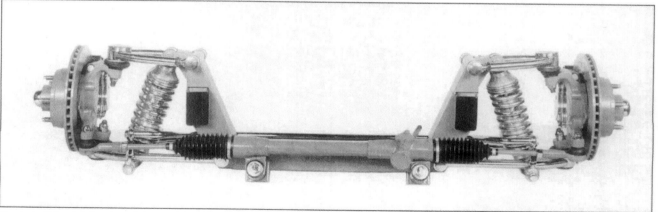

Designed for fat-fendered cars, this independent front suspension uses Mustang spindles, but without the Mustang cross-member or spring pockets. Coil-overs make for a cleaner, more compact assembly. *Heidt's*

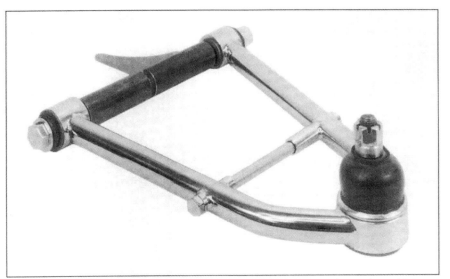

Stock Mustang II suspensions use a lower arm with a narrow pivot point, which necessitates an additional support strut. Most upgraded Mustang suspension kits utilize a lower arm with a wider stance so no additional strut is needed. *Heidt's*

for the street rod market and feature billet aluminum or tubular steel arms and polished coil-over shocks.

Heidt's, for example, offers their Superide, with upper and lower arms on each side supported by a nice coil-over shock assembly. This package comes with a cross-member that ties everything together. By using the coil-over shock-spring, the design eliminates the huge spring pocket seen on Mustang systems.

Kugel Komponents offers their Phase II independent front suspension. This system uses upper and lower arms, a coil-over on each side for support, and a cross-member designed to fit various hot rod frames. They also make independent suspension for

This close-up shows the Corvette suspension and front-steer rack-and-pinion used on the *Art Morrison MaxG* frame. *Art Morrison*

In order to achieve a perfect blend of form and function, Jerry Kugel has the control arms for his independent front suspension investment cast from 17-4 stainless steel. *Kugel Komponents*

Mustang independent front suspension systems are available with air bags instead of coil-over for the ultimate in adjustable suspension. *Heidt's*

cars with "pinched" frames, and a high-tech push-rod type of suspension that moves the coil-overs inboard in Formula One fashion.

Corvette components, both the latest C5 pieces and those from earlier models, are utilized in systems offered by Fat Man, Chassis Engineering, Mike Adams, and others. This makes it easy to use the latest Corvette suspension and brakes on both ends if you so desire. Gibbon Fiberglass and Chassis Engineering also offer torsion-bar front suspensions for 1935 to 1940 Ford cars.

Potential Problems

When buying a front suspension, whether it's a simple Mustang II unit or something more exotic, there are a few things to watch for.

First, a Mustang II system should use stock Ford geometry and the stock mounting position for the steering rack. Changing the position of the upper control arm or the length of the tie rods used with the Ford rack-and-pinion gear can lead to unpleasant consequences.

Second, there's a lot of unseen engineering that goes into any good front suspension. While you don't have to understand all the engineering, it makes good sense to buy from well-known companies. Ask the manufacturer or the dealer plenty of questions and don't sign the check until you're satisfied with their answers.

Third, when in doubt about what to buy, find someone at the next show with a suspension like the one you lust for, and ask them how it works in

the real world. Did the manufacturer provide good instructions? How hard was the system to install, and were they there to help with any questions that arose during the installation? Most rodders will be more than happy to discuss their experiences.

Riding on Air

This independent suspension section wouldn't be complete without an examination of the somewhat new air-ride systems. Most of these replace the spring(s) with an air bag from Goodyear or Firestone. The bags themselves are manufactured from the same two-ply material used to make the air bags seen on 18-wheel tractors and trailers. This whole technology is really a carryover from commercial trucks.

That's not to say all these air-suspension systems are the same. Some are designed from scratch to take advantage of the air bags, while others simply replace the spring in a Mustang II front suspension with an air bag. In all cases the bags themselves are connected to an air compressor controlled by a panel within the car.

Most independent suspension systems experience camber change as the suspension moves up-and-down. Many designs do this intentionally so that the outside tire tilts in and gets a better grip on the road as you roar around a curve. Yet, that camber change might not be such a good idea when you're dealing with suspension systems designed to operate over a wide range of ride heights.

When considering one of these air-bag designs,

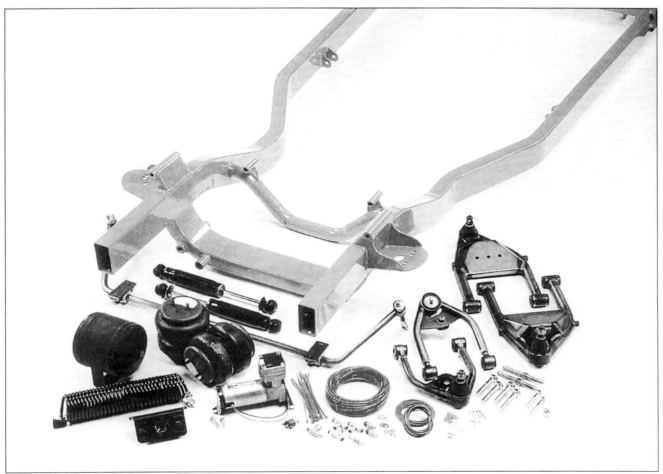

Here you see the components needed for the air suspension on this Art Morrison Air Spring Plus frame. Note the bags, compressor, reservoir, hardware, and the control arms designed to work within a wide range of possible heights.

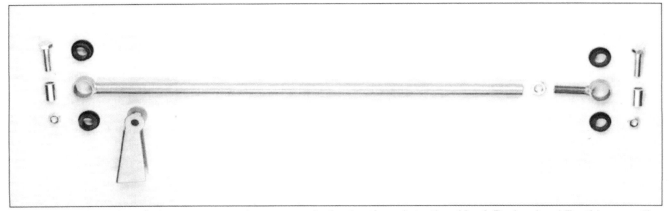

Cross-steer linkage installations can create bump steer by forcing the axle to the side. A Panhard rod like this one will ensure the axle only moves up-and-down, not side to side. *SO-CAL*

decide how much you're really going to utilize the height adjustment. Do you want to simply find a good ride height, close to a standard street rod ride height, and then lower the car when you park? Or do you want to be able to vary the usable ride height by 3 or 4 inches?

Systems designed from scratch around the air bags tend to offer the greatest height adjustment with the least amount of camber and toe-in change. Some offer a conventional bump stop so that if you pinch a line or let all the air out of the system, the suspension can't settle so far that any components are damaged. Others use bags that are designed with internal cushions that provide a final compression or rest stop.

The air-bag systems come to the table with a number of advantages and disadvantages. On the positive side, this technology allows the builder to set the car in the weeds for that really bitchin' profile, yet drive it home like any other car, crossing speed bumps with impunity. If you load the car with four friends and a small trailer out back, all you need to do to compensate is dial up a little more pressure and head out the driveway. Finally, air suspension is progressive (see Chapter Five for more on air springs). That is to say, the more the suspension is compressed, at a given pressure setting, the more it will resist further compression.

The cost of this new technology includes the cost (literally) of the pump and control unit, and any cost to retrofit one of these systems to an existing car. Cars with air bags are more complex and have more things to go wrong, but that may not be a consideration for many hot rodders. Ultimately these systems are best suited to fat fendered cars and trucks for one simple reason: the bags are ugly. There's no way to build an air bag that isn't black, or one with the aesthetic appeal of a polished coil-over.

Steering Linkage

Between the steering wheel and the two front tires is the steering linkage. Once again, there are a few options here that should be mentioned in the

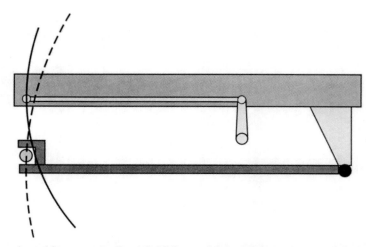

Many early rodders used a Ford F-100 or a Mustang box as part of their drag-link type of steering linkage. Trouble is, the typical Mustang box installation puts the pitman arm up, as shown, and creates poor geometry. Some of Pete and Jake's cars used a Mustang box and drag-link type of steering linkage, but with a four-bar linkage, which kept the axle and the outer end of the drag link moving in the same arc. *SO-CAL*

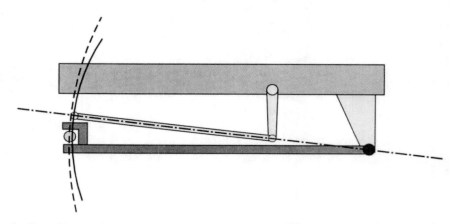

As Pete Chapouris says, "The early hot rods worked because they stayed close to stock Ford steering geometry [shown]. Unless you can keep the original engineering concept from Ford, the system doesn't work . . . the minute you put a lowered axle in there, no matter what you do it's never going to be right." *SO-CAL*

interest of making good decisions.

Cross-Steering for Dropped Axles

By far the most common style of steering linkage currently used with a dropped axle is the cross-steer system. This style of steering mounts the steering gear to the left frame rail. The drag link runs from the pitman arm, which is connected to the steering gear, across to the right-side steering arm.

What we call "bump steer" can occur with any type of steering linkage, usually because someone didn't take the time to think through the various components being used and how they interact as the suspension moves up-and-down. If, as the suspension compresses or extends, the steering linkage moves through a different arc than the axle itself (check the illustration) then you have essentially "steered" the vehicle. Axle movement, front to rear or side to side, can cause this problem.

In a car with a cross-steer linkage it's important to keep the tie rod and the drag link parallel, and the pitman arm pointing straight ahead when the gear is in the straight-ahead position (in the center of its movement). Worm-gear types of steering gears have a built-in "high point" at the very center of the movement. This is built in to compensate for any wear that might occur over time. The shaft of a properly adjusted steering gear will actually require slightly more torque to turn as it goes through this high point. In general, the Vega steering box (or the newly manufactured copies of it) is suitable for lighter-weight hot rods, such as Ford up to 1934. Larger cars, like fat-fendered Fords and GM cars, should use the slightly larger Saginaw 605 box, Saginaw 525 box, or equivalent.

Most street rod builders recommend the use of a Panhard rod with a dropped axle to avoid side-to-side movement of the axle as the car goes over bumps and around corners (see Pete Chapouris' comments earlier in this chapter). Installation of the Panhard rod must be considered carefully, however, so the axle and the drag link move through the same arcs. If in doubt, the builder can always call the company that manufactured the suspension parts for help with placement and installation of the Panhard rod.

When it comes to the steering linkage used with straight axles, there is a plan B. Early hot rods and a few bucket Ts use what's known as a drag-link style of linkage. This system positions the drag link on the left side of the car, connected between the steering gear and a left-side steering arm. Despite the fact that many old Indy roadsters ran exactly this type of linkage, it can be troublesome to install correctly. Unless the style of the car dictates a drag-link type of system, most builders are better off with a cross-steer linkage. Those who go ahead with linkage running on the car's left side need to take care that the axle doesn't experience any fore and aft movement as it moves up-and-down over a bump, and that the steering linkage is carefully laid out.

When it comes to deciding which type of steering to install in a solid axle car, Pete Chapouris is a

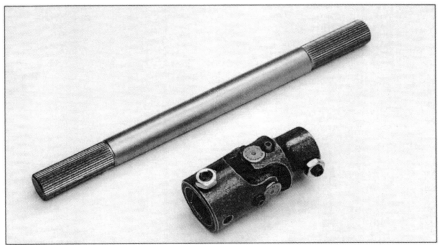

Steering shafts and the necessary U-joints are available as a kit like this one utilizing Borgeson U-joints. *SO-CAL*

big believer in the cross-steer, style of linkage: "To use the drag-link type of steering correctly it has to be laid out right," explains Pete. "With the Model A, the pivot points were in the general area of each other, but when people build cars like that now, there's just so many things that can go wrong. A lot of guys do it because of the nostalgia thing. But look at the old cars. The Pierson Brothers coupe is a cross-steer car, and that was built in 1949. When Henry started using cross-steer the hot rodders of the day followed suit. The cars we build at SO-CAL now, they all use cross-steer linkage, it's just so much better."

If this were a class or seminar, someone would be sure to raise a hand at this point and ask, "What about using a rack-and-pinion gear with a dropped axle?"

The answer is no. You can't. Well, you shouldn't use a rack-and-pinion with a dropped axle. Sure, we've all seen it done with varying degrees of success. That doesn't mean it's a good or a safe idea. First, the rack has to be mounted to the axle, then some kind of flexible link must be fashioned between the steering shaft and the gear which moves up-and-down with the axle. Not a good plan.

Where a rack does work extremely well is when it's used with an independent front suspension and the rack is *designed to work with that suspension system*. As mentioned before (but we'll mention it again) the rack and the suspension must be matched. In order to avoid bump steer, the ends of the tie rods must move through the same arcs as the control arms. This happens only when the two systems are designed from the start to work together—or someone has carefully matched an independent *suspension package* to a particular steering rack assembly.

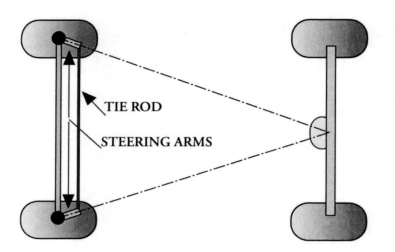

TIE ROD

STEERING ARMS

Above & Below: In a turn, all the tires must rotate around a common point. Because of the angle of the steering arms, the inside tire always turns in a little more sharply than the outside tire.

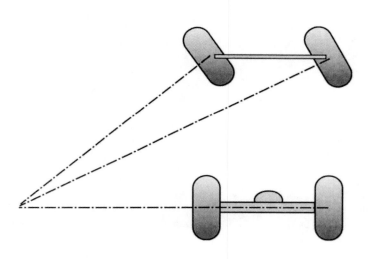

As the street rod industry matures and many of us drive bigger, heavier cars, the need arises for power steering. Not a problem you say—I'll just use the power version of that Ford rack-and-pinion and hook it up to the handy dandy GM power steering pump. The problem this time isn't geometry, but pressure, namely, the fact that the GM pump puts out way too much pressure for the stock Ford rack. Correctly solving the mismatch involves the use of a shim kit in the flow control valve, or an adjustable power steering valve from a company like Heidt's.

The conventional steering gears are often called worm-gears because of the shape of the internal gear. A good example and longtime favorite with street rodders is the Vega gear, now be-

ing remanufactured so you can purchase one brand-new. Another popular GM gear is the 525, a late-model manual gear that's just a bit bigger than the tried-and-true Vega gear. GM power steering gears can often be used in many typical cross-steer applications. Most of the steering gear mounting plates will accept either a manual or a power gear. The problem with power steering in cross-steer situations is the tight fit on the left side of most V-8s when installed in most street rod chassis.

This brings us back to the topic of mock-ups, already discussed in chapter 2. This concept definitely applies to the steering column and placement of the steering gear. In the case of a worm-style gear, the exhaust headers or manifold are often pretty close to the gear, whether it's power steering or not. You probably want to clamp or tack-weld the mounting plate for the steering gear to the frame, in what seems like the most logical location. Then install the engine and check the clearance between the shaft and gear, and the engine, mount, and exhaust.

In addition to good geometry, you need to consider the ergonomics. That is, the column should be mounted where it feels the most comfortable for the driver. With the column temporarily mounted, make sure the lower part of the column is high enough that you can move your foot from one pedal to the other without running into the column.

Next, locate the steering gear on the frame rail so that the shaft connecting the column to the gear is as straight as possible. With the wheels pointed straight ahead, the steering gear must be in the center of its movement. While many hot rod builders and shops position the gear so the pitman arm is parallel to the ground, that isn't necessary for good geometry and may make for a more complex linkage between the column and the steering gear.

Remember that it's easier to modify a header tube or change to a different style of exhaust manifold than it is to design a shaft with multiple U-joints and a support bearing. There are also a number of different pitman arms available for the most popular gears. These can be an aid in finding the ideal position for the gear, and will affect the gear's effective ratio and leverage; for instance, installing a longer pitman arm will make

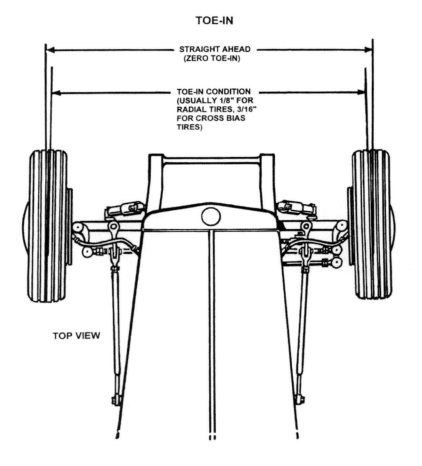

TOE-IN

STRAIGHT AHEAD (ZERO TOE-IN)

TOE-IN CONDITION (USUALLY 1/8" FOR RADIAL TIRES, 3/16" FOR CROSS BIAS TIRES)

TOP VIEW

Toe-in is very important to the way your car goes down the road. Too little or too much can make a car prone to wander, almost like insufficient positive caster. *SO-CAL*

and its bracket, will be magnified and result in loose and vague steering.

Among the parts you have to keep matched are the tapered ends of the tie-rod ends and the holes in the steering arm or pitman arm. Even similar appearing ends use different-diameter tapered studs, or studs with a different degree of taper. Because all the components that make up the steering linkage are so critical to your safety, be sure the taper and diameter of the tie-rod end matches perfectly the hole it fits into . . . and don't forget the cotter key.

Mounting a Rack-and-Pinion Gear

While some older independent front suspensions use a cross-steer system, the majority of newer IFS set-ups use a rack-and-pinion. The position of the rack-and-pinion is determined by the supplier of the front suspension kit. Some are "front steer" and some are "rear steer," meaning the gear assembly is mounted to the front or rear of the front cross-member. As the position of the rack affects the overall geometry, changes to the position of the rack should be avoided. Stick with the position of the rack as determined by the engineers at Ford Motor Company, or Kugel, or the manufacturer of the front suspension kit.

As discussed in the illustration on alignment, the shape and angle of the steering arms creates the effect known as toe-out on turns. The angle of the arms is critical. Don't use the heat-wrench to reshape them and solve a clearance problem.

the steering quicker. Though the U-joint manufacturers say the joints will work at angles up to 25 or 30 degrees, a smaller angle is always better.

The U-joints you use for the steering shaft must be high-quality needle-bearing U-joints. There are less expensive U-joints out there that do not use needle bearings to support the cross-shaft. These are generally meant for industrial applications and have no place in your steering shaft assembly. Borgeson and various dealers sell complete kits with U-joints and a shaft, as well as vibration dampeners and collapsible shafts for safety. Support bearings and brackets for three-joint shafts are available as well.

The mounting plate used for the steering gear must be well mounted, preferably welded, to the frame rail. Even a very miniscule amount of flex between the bracket and the frame, or the gear

Things To Do

It seems this chapter is full of "don'ts" and things to avoid. Rather than leave you on a negative note, we've decided to finish with some of the things that you should do: Buy only quality parts and kits from known suppliers. Take your time when you're doing suspension work. Think your way through each step to avoid making dumb mistakes. Have fun and *be proud of the work* you've done.

The cowl-mounting hole is the reference point used by Joe in determining the correct place to put the front cross-member. It's a good idea, though, to double-check the position of the cross-member using other reference points.

*T*his demonstration was done in the Kugel shop by Joe Kugel, one of the two Kugel sons who do much of the day-to-day running of the shop founded by their father, Jerry Kugel. This sequence starts at the very beginning with the installation of the cross-member.

At Kugel, all the measurements start with one reference, the front body-mounting hole or the cowl-mounting hole. They measure 17.25 inches forward from the center of the cowl-mounting hole to find the axle center line on this 1935–1940 Ford frame.

As Joe explains, "I go 17 1/4 inches forward from the center of the mounting hole, then add 1/4

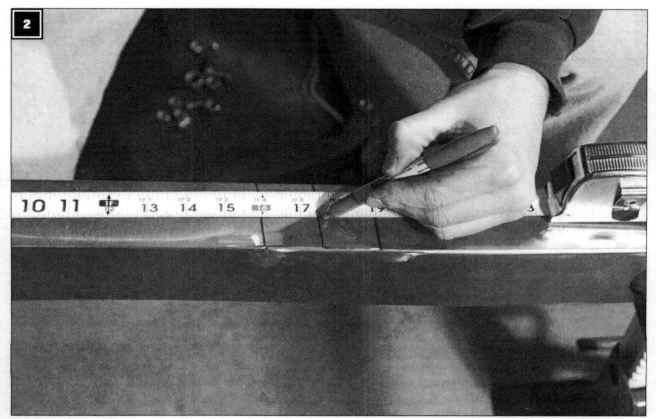

Joe measures 17 1/4 inches forward to determine the standard axle centerline, then moves that point 1/4 inch farther forward to compensate for the effect of positive caster. The position of the cross-member is marked with a marker, not by scribing the frame rail.

With help from a floor jack, Joe positions the cross-member between the frame rails. Note the straps tack-welded across the very front of the rails.

After carefully tack-welding the cross-member in place, it's time to position the upper pivots. The left- and right-side pivots are not interchangeable.

Joe is careful to position the pivots correctly—a mistake at this point will make it difficult or *impossible to get the* alignment correct later.

inch, and that's the center of the front cross-member. We add a quarter inch because by the time they get the correct caster, it pushes the spindle back slightly." Next he marks the frame rails 1 1/2 inches on either side of the adjusted centerline, because the cross-member is 3 inches wide. This particular installation uses SAC (Specialized Auto Components) Hot Rod Products' rails for a 1940 Ford truck (the 1935–1940 Ford frames are all the same).

Joe likes to double-check the centerline against other reference points. The SAC rails have the rear-axle centerline stamped, so he can measure forward from that mark, and do a cross-measurement as well.

With everything marked, it's time to tack-weld the cross-member in place. "You have to be careful that the cross-member doesn't move as you do the tack-welds," warns Joe, "and it's important to move around from side to side as you do the actual

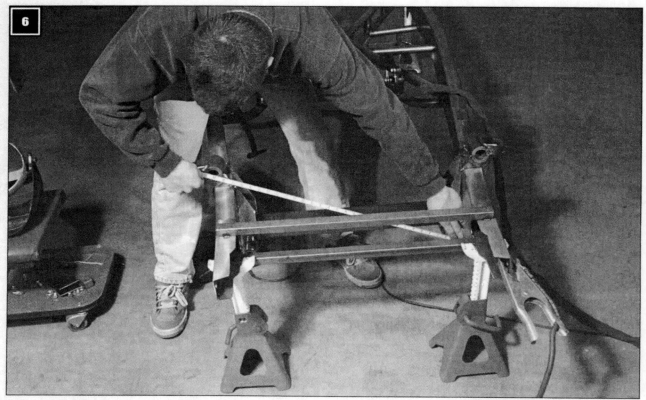

Before doing the final welding of the cross-member and pivots, Joe does a cross-measurement check to be absolutely sure the parts are positioned correctly. With the frame at ride-rake, a protractor can be used to ensure that the cross-member is positioned correctly front to rear.

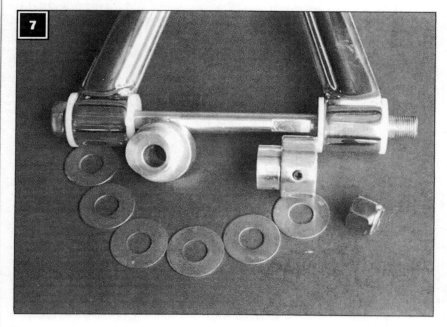

The eccentrics seen here are affixed to the upper-arm pivot shaft with set screws. By turning the shaft both eccentrics move, thus affecting the camber. The shims are used to move the arm front to rear and thus set the caster. Kugel upper and lower arms are investment cast stainless *steel*.

The assembly of the front suspension starts with the installation of the lower arm, held in position by this simple strut.

Joe has assembled the spindle and rotor and now sets the whole thing in place on the lower ball joint.

finish welding, so you don't concentrate too much heat in one area and cause warpage."

Next he sets the upper A-arm pivots in place; these are separate pieces of the cross-member. Joe shows me the difference in the two parts, and emphasizes the fact that these are not interchangeable from side to side. Once they are both tacked in place, Joe does a series of double-checks to make sure they are positioned correctly. As he explains, "If they are off very much, you probably won't get the alignment within specifications." He also does a cross-measurement to ensure they are square.

Now we install the actual front-end components for the Phase II independent front suspension. The upper and lower arms are investment cast, 17-4, heat-treated stainless steel. This suspension uses a rear-steer rack-and-pinion gear.

Joe installs the lower arm first, and a temporary strut is used to hold it in position. The Kugel front end shown here uses eccentrics, two per upper arm, for alignment. The eccentrics are turned to adjust the camber. Shims are used to move the upper arm ahead or back and thus change the caster angle.

This kit's spindle assemblies are cast from 17-4 stainless as well, and Joe installs the spindles next. In this case the rotor and *caliper are already in*

Next he installs the eccentrics prior to the installation of the upper arm.

The upper pivot arm goes in last. Once the arm is in place, the set screws in each eccentric will be tightened against the flats machined on each pivot shaft.

place, though you could certainly install just the bare spindle assembly. The upper arm and eccentrics come next. Joe points out the importance of properly assembling the upper arm assemblies. "People need to realize that the set screws should be tightened against the shaft. That way both of them move at once when the shaft is turned—and you will correctly adjust the camber."

Joe does in fact do a camber check with a magnetic camber gauge, explaining, "You need to be close to ride height to do this, with the temporary shock-strut in place. Then check the camber. This can be done with a protractor as well. Builders should check the camber before they do the final welding. Also, as a good caster check before the final welding is done, we tell them that the front cross-member should be level, or kicked back 1 degree with the frame at the ride rake."

An old-fashioned magnetic camber and caster gauge is used to do a rough camber adjustment and ensure that the cross-member and related components are positioned correctly. A protractor could be used for this as well.

Though a sway bar is available for this front end, Joe did not install one at this time.

The finished installation, complete with steering rack, seen in a very similar frame at the *Kugel facility*.

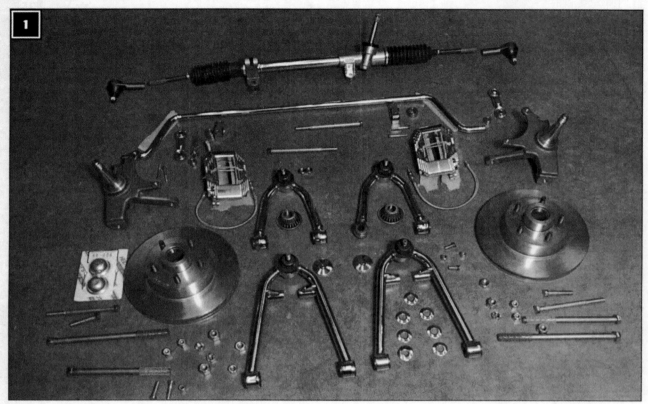

It's a good idea to start the assembly by first spreading everything out on the floor or the bench. The Heidt's kit used here includes stainless upper and lower arms and dropped spindles.

This sequence continues the construction of a fairly typical street rod chassis for a Deuce pickup truck, the same chassis we saw in chapter 2. The front suspension used here is the Superide system from Heidt's suspension. In the next sequence, we've also included a front-suspension installation sequence photographed at the Kugel Komponents shop.

The Components

This Heidt's kit includes upper and lower arms made from polished stainless steel. The assorted hardware that comes with this kit is polished stainless as well. In order to achieve the ride height they want, Neal and John decided to use Heidt's 2-inch dropped spindles. They made this decision regarding the spindles after discussing the project with the technicians at Heidt's. As Neal explains, "Heidt's suggested the 2-inch dropped spindle would put the truck where we want it, based on what we said about the rake and ride height we want and the tire sizes."

The first step, and perhaps the most important one, is the installation of the front cross-member, already covered in chapter 2. It's a good idea to lay out all the parts on the floor, simply to ensure you have all of them, and that you understand what bolts to what. By putting all the parts in one neat grouping, you also make it less likely that you will forget to install one part or one bolt.

With the cross-member in place, Neal goes ahead and installs the steering rack, which mounts in straightforward fashion to the mounts that are part of the cross-member. Next come the lower control arms, which bolt to the mounts on the cross-member. Neal now bolts the lower shock mount to the lower control arm with the supplied hardware. The shocks came from Heidt's. These are adjustable for rebound damping, and include the springs recommended by Heidt's for this particular vehicle. It's important to face the shocks so that the adjustment knob is as accessible as possible. The upper arms bolt on next, followed by the dropped spindles.

When installing the front suspension for the last time, be sure to get the nuts tight enough that the tapered male part of the ball joints are drawn

The front cross-member is already installed, so Neal can go ahead and install the steering rack, which bolts to brackets that are part of the cross-member.

With the rack in place Neal installs the lower arms first.

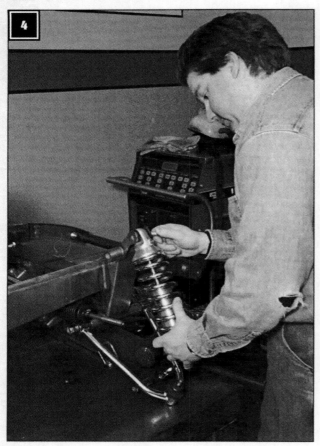

Installation of the adjustable front shock absorbers comes next.

This part of the assembly is pretty straightforward. After installing the lower arm and coil-over, Neal positions the upper arm and slides the upper pivot bolt in place.

up fully into the matching female hole in the spindle assembly. Conversely, if you're just doing a mock-up, avoid pulling the pins up too tight, as they can take a set and be hard to remove. The trick to disassembly after the pin is fully drawn up into the spindle is to hold one hammer head on one side of the female spindle assembly while rapping the other side. This will "pop" the tapered pin out of the hole. Don't be tempted to whack the tapered stud itself, as damage to the threads is sure to result. You can also rent or buy a "pickle fork" that will do the same thing.

Once all the suspension arms and the spindle assemblies are in place, it's time to install the rotors. As mentioned elsewhere, if you've never packed and installed a set of wheel bearings before, ask for help. Most garages have special tools or adapters for the grease gun that force the grease up between the individual rollers. It doesn't hurt to put a bit of grease on the outer bearing races as

well. If the rotors come without the bearing races installed, be sure to use the correct driver during the installation and be sure the races are fully seated in the hub. The grease you use must be rated for wheel-bearing use on cars with disc brakes. When tightening the nut for the wheel bearings, be sure to follow the recommendations in a good service manual so they don't end up too tight or too loose.

Most of these suspension kits and assemblies come with their own instructions, which may include a quick wheel alignment check. Remember that the car needs to be at ride height before you check the alignment. Camber can be checked easily by placing a digital level or angle gauge on the rotor or hub surface. The caster angle, however, can be hard to check on a car with independent suspension if you don't have access to the turn plates that are part of a good alignment rack.

Installing the sway bar for this kit involves drilling two holes into the frame on either side. These holes are used to mount the two pillow blocks that locate the sway bar. In the case of the Heidt's Superide, the sway bar needs to be

The Heidt's system uses threaded collars at either end of the upper arm to adjust both camber and caster. Note the adjustment knob at the upper end of the Aldan shock, used to control rebound damping.

installed before the front end is fully assembled, something Neal discovered the hard way (which is why it's a good idea to assemble most of these components twice, once during the mock-up and once for the final assembly). Also of note, the threads on the end of the sway bar were damaged slightly during shipping—that's why it's nice to have a tap and die set in the tool box.

What's left is the installation of the anti-sway bar, seen here mounted in the two pillow blocks behind the cross-member, with the links tying it to the lower coil-over mounting bolt.

Once the upper and lower arms, coil-overs, and anti-sway bar are in place, the front suspension is essentially installed. Installing front rotors and calipers will be covered in the brake chapter.

Chapter 4

Rear Suspension

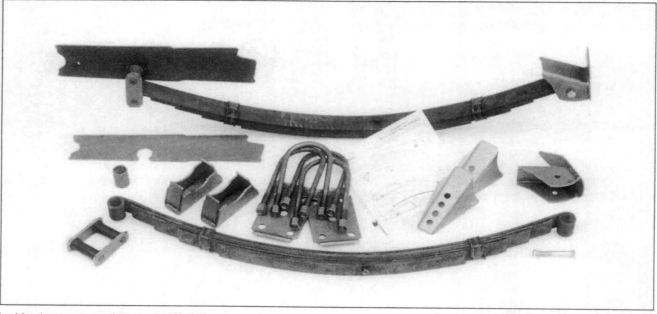

Ladder bars, as used on many SO-CAL cars and sold in kit form, make a nice, simple, functional rear suspension that works with either a buggy spring or a pair of coil-overs.

We emphasized in chapter 3 the importance of the front suspension. That doesn't mean the rear suspension is *unimportant*, or that you shouldn't give careful consideration to the type of rear suspension that best suits your new rod. Many roadsters leave the rear suspension open to view, which means the rear suspension can be an important part of the car's visual package. Even if yours is a fat-fendered car with a mostly invisible rear axle, the linkage, springs, and the rear-end assembly itself certainly contribute to the ride, handling, and ride height of the car.

A discussion of independent versus solid rear axles runs parallel to the discussion of front axles. An independent rear suspension provides better handling and ride (in most situations). The downside is cost and mechanical complexity.

While the high zoot cars in the magazines might have a fully independent and polished

rear suspension from Kugel, or a converted Corvette or Jaguar system, that doesn't mean you can't install a solid Ford 9-inch rear end with coil or leaf springs. Literally millions of cars and thousands of hot rods are motoring around today on nothing more sophisticated than a solid rear axle, two springs, and the linkage necessary to keep it all in place.

Solid Axle Options

A solid rear axle can be supported in a variety of ways: two parallel leaf springs, a single transverse buggy spring, a pair of coils, or a pair of air bags. Henry Ford liked the buggy spring, used on most of his cars up to 1948. Today, that option is less popular, though the kits and components available from SO-CAL (and a few others) are making the buggy spring a more viable rear suspension choice than ever before.

Before deciding which is the best suspension option for your solid rear axle, consider the options.

Leaf Springs

Though low in sex appeal, there's nothing wrong with leaf springs. They're durable and readily available and make a good suspension, especially under heavier, fatter cars. Spring assemblies like those from Posies come with slippery, synthetic buttons under the end of each leaf to minimize internal "stiction," one of the inherent disadvantages of leaf springs.

Another way to eliminate friction from within the spring pack is to eliminate the pack and use a single leaf. There seem, however, to be some problems with these products and many have been withdrawn from the market.

Height adjustment is difficult at best with leaf springs. Sure, you can always use lowering

Installation of a quick-change rear end in a Deuce frame requires the use of a Model A–style rear cross-member. *SO-CAL*

blocks like the kids did on their 1952 Fords, but wouldn't it be better to buy the right spring the first time? In order to lower the rear of the car, some rodders pull one or more leafs from the spring pack. Before following suit, however, consider that all those leafs in the pack were designed to work together. The best solution is to ask the person who manufactures the spring or rear suspension kit whether or not the springs have been de-arched and what the ride height will be when the springs are used with a car like yours. In a case where the spring is already chosen and the rear of the car sits too high, a good spring shop can de-arch a leaf spring assembly or reverse the eyes to lower the car.

Coil Springs

Often the suspension of choice for early cars, coil-spring rear suspensions come in many different forms. Coil springs are used in at least four different styles of rear suspension, each with certain advantages and disadvantages.

The straight and simple parallel four-bar might be the best known of the coil-spring rear suspension systems; four-bar kits are available from every major street rod manufacturer and catalog company. Just weld the brackets to the rear end, another set of brackets to the frame, connect with the four links, and add coils or coil-overs. Like all rear suspension kits, installing the four-bar suspension will require that you carefully set up the rear end at ride height before welding on the four-bar brackets. One big advantage of a four-bar is that there is no pinion-angle change as the suspension moves

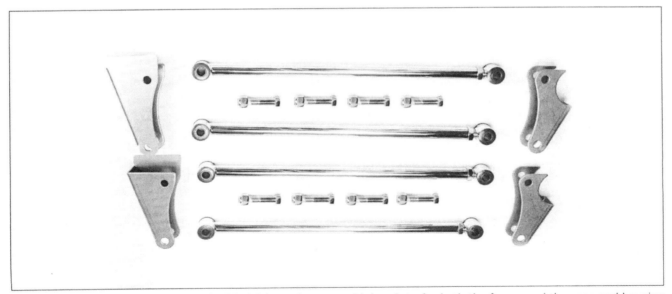

This parallel four-bar kit is designed for Model As and comes with brackets for both the frame *and the rear end housing.* It's available in standard steel or stainless. *Deuce Factory*

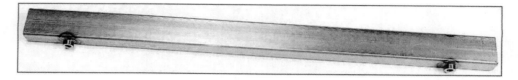

You can simplify frame construction with the use of this rectangular rear cross-member. Made from 0.120-wall-thickness mild steel tubing, the mounting bungs for coil-over shocks are already installed. *Deuce Factory*

At SO-CAL they like to weld the ladder bar brackets on to the rear end housing (with the housing in a fixture) then send it out for the installation of the ends and straightening of the housing.

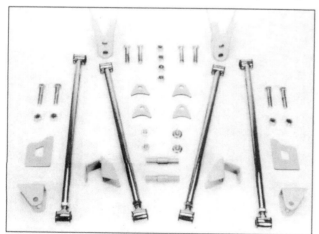

Available to fit many cars, this triangulated four-bar needs no Panhard rod, and comes with standard or stainless four-bars. *Chassis Engineering*

through its travel (just as a four-bar front end has no caster change).

As mentioned elsewhere in this book, welding on the rear end housing generally warps the housing, which must be checked and repaired by a qualified shop after the brackets are installed.

Unlike some other coil-spring rear suspension systems, the parallel four-bar system needs a Panhard rod to eliminate side-to-side axle movement. This means there's *one more bracket* to bolt or weld to the axle housing, and the need for a matching bracket on the frame.

To eliminate the Panhard rod, some builders use a triangulated four-bar system. This arrangement positions two of the bars parallel to the car's axis like a standard four-bar system. The other two bars, however, are mounted at an angle so they can absorb side loads and eliminate the need

This close-up shows the built-in sway bar and triangulated rear suspension used with the MaxG chassis. *Art Morrison*

for a Panhard rod. The problem is the way the angled bars sometimes get in the way of the exhaust system as it snakes its way to the rear of the car. And though there are thousands of these out there in use, some builders don't like the way the lower and upper links move in different planes, which puts the upper bars in a bind when the suspension moves up-and-down.

Ladder bars, another option in the coil-spring world, are about as simple as a suspension system gets. Welded to the axle housing, each "ladder" runs well forward and connects to brackets and a cross-member near the middle of the chassis. Roy Brizio states that they often use ladder bars on the cars they build in their shop, and for good reason. "With ladder bars you bring all the torque to the center of the car, and the torque acts on the center of mass, the way Henry liked it."

A ladder bar system requires a Panhard rod when coil springs are used, and the bars can get in the way of a dual exhaust system. The rear end supported by ladder bars also experiences pinion-angle change as the suspension moves up-and-down, in much the same way a split wishbone

Ladder bars, as used on many SO-CAL cars and sold in kit form, make a nice, simple, functional rear suspension that works with either a buggy spring or a pair of coil-overs.

73

Based on the 9-inch Ford, this assembly uses its own rear cross-member and stainless components and is available in various widths. *Kugel Komponents*

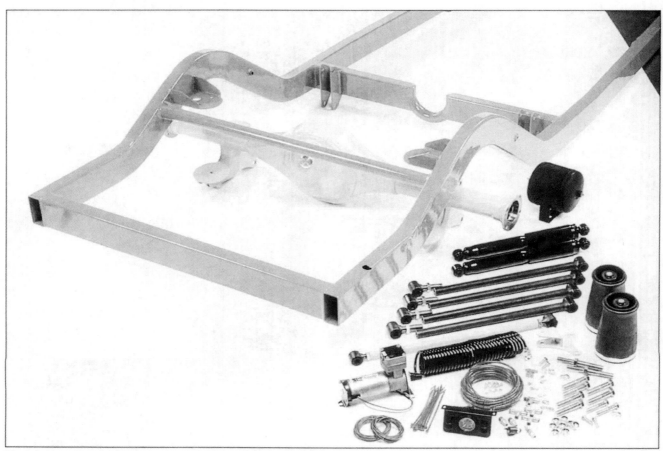

The air bags used for rear suspension are slightly different than those used on the front. The system shown here from Art Morrison is intended to be used with its own frame. *Art Morrison*

front suspension experiences caster change as the wheel goes over a bump.

The final installment in this coil-spring suspension treatise is a seldom used suspension called a three-bar. Think of a parallel four-bar system without the top bars. Now add one shorter, upper link and a Panhard rod. Simpler than a four-bar, the three-bar provides good traction and a good launch, and is often seen on true drag-race cars. The Deuce pickup illustrated in the In the Shop sequences in this chapter uses just such a system.

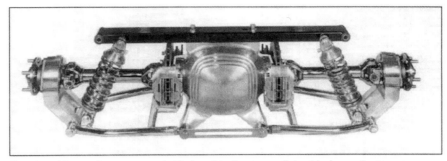

For the ultimate in sex appeal, it's hard to beat a polished independent rear suspension. Available in various widths, this assembly is based on the Ford 9-inch rear end and comes with its own cross-member for ease of installation. *Heidt's*

Act Independently

The street rod and hot rod industry has grown tremendously in the past 10 or 15 years. Nowhere is that growth more apparent than in the wide range of independent rear suspensions available for the typical hot rod.

Not long ago the options list here included mostly the converted Corvette or Jaguar rear suspension systems. A few of the catalogs offered kits that made it possible to convert one of the systems to street rod use. Boyd Coddington's shop took the Corvette independent system to a new plateau and made it their own. Today, independent rear suspensions come in as many flavors as ice cream. Kugel, Heidt's, and Dutchman are just three of the companies that manufacture complete stand-alone independent suspension systems based on the Ford 9-inch rear end.

These rear suspension systems were designed from the start to be installed in your hot rod. If you're afraid that the torque of a street Hemi or 502-ci Chevy will spit those Jaguar spider gears out onto the pavement, try a bulletproof Ford 9-inch as the foundation of a very trick independent rear suspension system. Now add axles available in various lengths, connected to heavy-duty U-joints, supported by trick cast or billet aluminum supports.

This is Yankee ingenuity at its best. Extremely durable, these independent rear suspensions come as a complete assembly with their own subframe, ready for installation into the chassis of your choice.

If the stand-alone assemblies seem a bit expensive or you like to get your hands really dirty and do everything yourself, a number of companies offer kits that allow the adaptation of Corvette rear suspensions to street rod use. Chassis Engineering offers trailing arms and cross-members to install pre-C5 Corvette suspension components in a

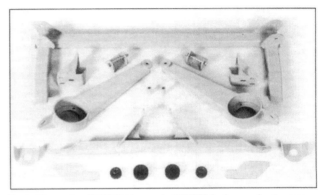

Early Corvette (1963 through 1979) independent rear suspension can be adapted to many cars with kits that include the main cross-member, trailing arms, and necessary brackets. *Chassis Engineering*

variety of hot rods. Fat Man makes complete rear subframes to convert C5 (late-model) Corvette components to nearly any hot rod application. Art Morrison, too, has Corvette suspension kits meant for hot rods.

No matter which style of rear suspension you install, independent or solid axle, you should consider the position of the wheel in the rear fender opening (assuming there are rear fenders). Some fat-fendered cars use an axle centerline from the factory that positions the rear wheel slightly to the front of the fender opening, which means you probably want to move the centerline back slightly. This is another reason to spend time with the car mocked-up in the shop with the chassis at ride height.

If you buy a rear suspension kit, ask the manufacturer where in the fenderwell their kit positions the rear wheel. Or, follow the example of builder Steve Moal, who likes to roll the mock-up outside so he can stand back and really assess how the car "sits" and how all the parts work together.

A pair of struts take the place of the shocks during the mock-up and installation of the rear suspension.

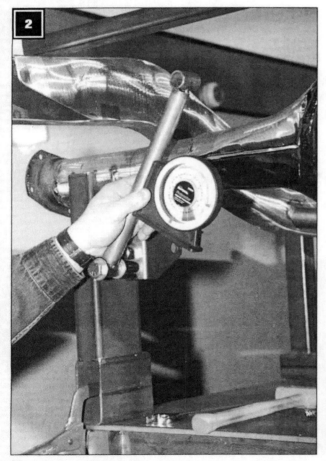

Neal designed the upper and lower mounts to put the shock at a 30-degree angle, which is the recommendation from Aldan. All of this depends on the ride height determined during the mock-up stage.

*W*e continue to document the construction of the stretched Deuce truck. This installment presents the installation of the rear axle and three-bar suspension with coil-over shocks.

The installation of the rear end and suspension really started when Neal and John did the mock-up on the truck. That's when they decided how much rake the truck needed, how tall the tires would be, and ultimately, where the rear end would sit. The suspension to be used on this Deuce pickup is a three-bar, supported by coil-over shocks mounted behind the axle housing.

Neal suggests that two of the major considerations affecting the location of the rear end and the installation of the suspension is "the amount of travel you want the rear end to have, and how much room there is for the shocks."

When it comes to choosing the correct springs, you can weigh the car, figure the angle of the shocks, and then use charts and graphs to determine the necessary spring rate. Neal took the easy way out by calling Aldan and asking them for a recommendation, which they gave as 250 lb/in based on the wheelbase, the engine, and the capacity of the fuel tank. "But before I called Aldan," explains Neal, "I already knew I would have a total of 3 inches of travel and that the shock would be 13 inches long from eye to eye when fully extended. I determined those dimensions during the mock-up, but if I'd needed help Deuce Factory can provide some recommendations as well."

Like most shock absorber manufacturers, Aldan makes shocks with various types of attaching

The upper shock mounts are part of the rear crossmember, made up from square tubing and cut to just slide between the frame rails.

The cross-member must be installed evenly from side to side, and located so the upper and lower shock mounts are perfectly parallel.

Before tack-welding it into place, Neal makes sure the cross-member is level both from side to side, and front to back.

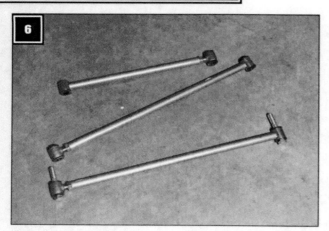

These are mild steel mock-ups of the links that will be swapped later for stainless replacements. Even though the links will be replaced, they are the same length and made from the same 3/16-inch wall, 7/8-inch tubing used for the final stainless links.

points on either end. The pair installed here have urethane bushings on either end, and metal sleeves inside each bushing. The flexible bushings will compensate for minor misalignment of the two supporting pins, and the urethane makes a high-quality, silent bushing.

Based on the suggestions from Aldan, Neal installed the shocks at a 30-degree angle, with the frame and axle at ride height. Aldan also recommends that the shocks be one-third of the way compressed when the vehicle is at ride height. In Neal's case, the suspension has 3 inches of travel—from ride height to the end of travel (on compression) is 2 inches, while from ride height to the end of travel on extension is 1 inch.

The Aldan shocks are their model 654 with adjustments for rebound damping, as well as for ride height. Neal plans to install a simple conical rubber snubber on either side to provide a positive stop to suspension movement.

Mounting the suspension links is made easier with the rear end and frame mounted on the

Neal shows the eventual location of the Panhard rod; it will mount lower because there's no upper suspension link on the left side. "The bar should be level at ride height, with equal travel up and down," says Neal. "That way the housing doesn't move side-to-side when the suspension goes up and down."

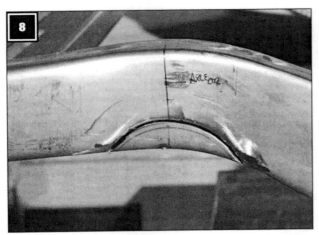

In order to match the ride height and suspension travel, it will be necessary to notch the frame. Neal made a template from light board (not shown), marked the frame, and then cut it out with a cut-off wheel.

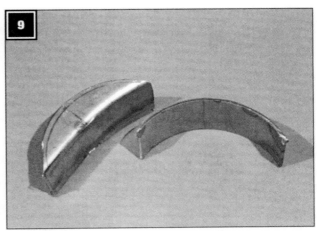

The filler piece was formed from flat mild steel plate the same thickness as the frame rails, though Neal suggests that "for a lot of people, a piece of large-diameter pipe would be better because it's already formed."

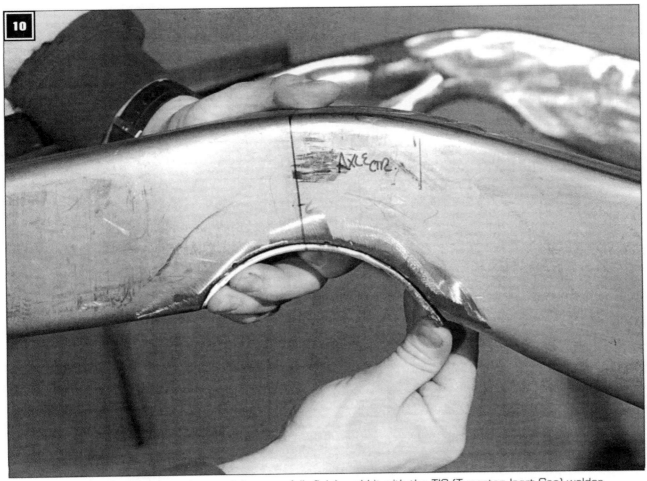

Neal will tack-weld the filler into place and then carefully finish weld it with the TIG (Tungsten Inert Gas) welder.

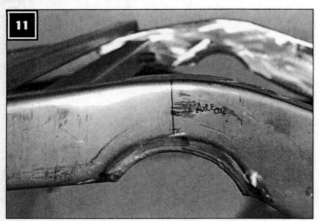

The finished C-section is 1 inch deep, twice as deep as Neal needed to get the correct amount of movement on compression. "The deeper C will allow me to put a rubber snubber up in the apex of the C," explains Neal.

table at ride height. Once Neal determined the pinion angle (more later), he could lay out the two lower links and the single upper link. The lower bars are made up from tubing just for the mock-up, but they are the same length as standard, off-the-shelf four-bar links. By using standard dimensions, it's easy to buy polished stainless links for the final assembly. With everything in the jig, Neal was able to tack-weld tabs to the axle housing and then install the temporary lower links, and thus determine where the front mounting brackets should go. "I put the brackets and bars inside the frame rail; normally people install them on the bottom of the frame rail," explains Neal. "This way they're a little higher and they also don't interfere with the installation of the running boards."

The shorter upper link is mounted on the right side of the axle housing. Like the lower links, this shorter link will be replaced with a stainless link, though the finished upper link will

With the C-sections finished, Neal is able to put the axle housing back into place and weld up the pivot points for the three-bar suspension links.

The rear shocks are model 654 from Aldan, adjustable for rebound damping and for ride height, equipped with a 250-lb/in spring. The lower mount acts as a spacer so the spring doesn't hit the rear end housing, and also spreads out the load of the lower mount.

To install the rear shocks, it helps to put the frame on jack stands and then use the floor jack to get the lower mount to a height that matches the position of the lower eye on the shock

be made up special by Deuce Factory from the same heavy-wall stainless tubing used for the standardized lower links.

One of the things that Neal likes about the three-bar is the way it allows more room for the Panhard rod and the exhaust. Neal shows how, with a standard four-bar setup, the Panhard rod would have to be mounted higher, so it won't run into the upper link on the left side. Because this three-bar suspension uses no upper link on the left side, the Panhard rod can be mounted lower so there's no chance it will contact the floor of the pickup box.

For mounting hardware, Neal plans to use stainless bolts on the lower links because, he says, "These are loaded in double-shear, so there isn't much load on the bolt itself. Some of the other bolts, like the upper mounting bolts for the shocks, are essentially loaded in single-shear and those will be chrome, grade-8 bolts. For the nuts I like Nyloc so I know they won't back off." (See the hardware chapter for a discussion of double-shear, single-shear, and the issues surrounding stainless bolts.)

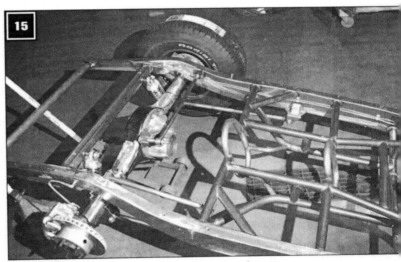

The finished suspension, minus the suspension stops and the final stainless links. Mounting points on the frame are built from 3/16-inch plate. Lower links have been moved in from their more common position in order to keep them higher and out of the way of the running boards.

Anyone familiar with the typical SO-CAL chassis might think that the only rear suspension they use is a buggy spring supporting a 9-inch Ford rear end.

In reality SO-CAL offers both buggy and coil spring rear suspensions designed to handle either a Ford 9-inch or a quick-change Halibrand rear end.

The most popular of the rear suspension options at SO-CAL is the buggy spring matched up to a Ford 9-inch rear end. Though you can buy the frame bare and install the rear suspension yourself, most buyers are money ahead to let SO-CAL set up the rear end and chassis. To quote Shane again, "You could buy all the brackets and weld them onto the 9-inch housing, but I don't recommend that. You spend a ton of time getting the brackets centered, the pinion angle right, and the shocks set correctly. All of that is already set on the jigs we use to set up the rear end.

"A total of eight parts have to be welded to the rear end housing. If you have any of those off a little, you create a bind, or too much pinion angle. We start with the bare housing with no ends, and weld the brackets on with the housings in a jig. Then the housings go to Currie, where they are straightened and the ends are welded on with the housing in their jig. It's a lot of work but the results are a perfectly straight housing. It's much better to go with the kit, it's engineered to go together. It's a bolt together deal."

Owners of SO-CAL cars report that the buggy spring rear suspension works really well, a testament to all the work that Pete and Shane put into the program. Another well-known street rod builder, Roy Brizio, once stated, "a buggy spring works great, but only if it's exactly the right spring." The buggy springs used in the back of a SO-CAL car are made specially to their specifications. "Basically," explains Shane, "we started with a '40 Ford spring that we had tweaked, one that was in a car that rode really well. We took that to a spring company and they used it as the template, so what we get is a custom spring."

Before the spring goes into a car, the crew at SO-CAL grinds and details each individual leaf so there are no sharp corners or rough edges. The leafs are powder coated and the assembly is greased between the leafs so there is no harshness to the ride.

The detailing doesn't stop there. "We always set the suspension up so the shackles are at a 45-degree angle," explains Shane. "That way they don't need a Panhard rod. Guys who want to race around corners might still need one, but the spring has the shackles in tension which pretty much eliminates the need for the Panhard rod."

The typical SO-CAL setup requires "C-ing" the frame and provides 3 1/2 inches of travel between the housing and the snubber. The springs are installed with a 1- or 1 1/2-inch spacer between the spring and the frame, in order to get the back end of the highboys up high enough. Of course, for someone who wants the car really low, that spacer can be removed.

Shane's final words of advice to home builders includes a warning to check that the rear end is centered and square in the chassis. "They need to make sure that the rear end is square in the car. When putting in ladder bars, you need to measure diagonally from either side of the housing up to the center of the front cross-member. Lots of people don't do that and the rear end is cocked and then the car doesn't go straight down the road. The other thing to watch out for is whether or not the lower shock stud positions the shock far enough away from the axle housing. We've seen some installations where the shock hits the axle housing, so now we've had our own, longer, lower shock stud manufactured."

When asked about the pros and cons of the venerable Halibrand rear end, Shane described it as "an awesome product that is now available on a timely basis. I just ordered one and it's here today. The noise is an issue but it can be greatly diminished by using their helical-cut gears instead of the straight-cut gears.

"In the past Pete would always take spare parts when he took one of these cars on the road. After all, the rear ends were originally designed for roundy-round cars. But now the reliability is pretty good."

*"H*ave fun while you work" might be a phrase coined for, or by, Jerry Kugel. The man running the well-known Kugel Komponents shop admits that he "gets a little bored on the weekends" when he doesn't come in to the shop. The shop itself isn't huge, just big enough for Jerry, his two sons, and one or two additional employees. Neat as a pin, the Kugel work space houses a variety of hot rod chassis under construction, a group of display chassis with Kugel front suspensions on them, a work area where Jerry assembles the independent rear suspensions, and one corner for their Bonneville car. Jerry says that as time goes on he turns more and more of the business over to his two sons, Jeff and Joe. Most business founders in Jerry's position, with competent sons to run the successful business, would be looking at retirement. That may not be a likely option for Jerry, however, simply because he's still having way too much fun at Kugel Komponents to give it all up.

Q. Jerry, can you give us a little history on the shop and tell us how you came to be one of the best-known manufacturers of street rod suspensions?

A. Well, I started in 1960, as a mechanic, and then in 1969 I started my own shop doing general repair. I always liked the hot rods and I always did some of that work in the shop. By 1975 the work in the shop was 50/50, or half hot rod work. In 1983 I sold the garage and went into street rodding full time. I was always into suspension work. I built my first car, a Deuce with Jaguar suspension front and rear, in 1970.

After doing that first car I started putting suspensions in for other people, and we always used the Jag components. By the early 1980s, I decided I wanted to build my own fully-independent front end assembly. It was all stainless and I was the first one on the block to make a complete assembly like that and sell it to street rodders and builders.

Q. Why did you first use Jaguar components?

A. In the late 1960s there wasn't much to choose from, most of the OEM stuff from Detroit had ugly stamped A-arms. The Jaguar stuff was better looking. It used unequal-length A-arms and had camber change as the suspension went through its range of motion, so it had good geometry. Jaguar used the same system in their race cars of the day. You could adapt the XKE suspension to a hot rod easily, and I thought it looked nice. When I decided to do my own system I used geometry similar to the Jag's because that's what I'm accustomed to and I know it works.

Q. Why have you chosen to cast your parts from stainless instead of having them cut out of billet aluminum?

A. You can cast stainless like we do [lost wax or investment casting] and you have very little machining. You don't have to spend all that time cutting a piece out of billet; the labor rates are such that this method works better for us. There's so much precision in the part when it's first cast that we only have to do very minimal machining. We try to build everything in-house, the only thing we don't do is the casting, which is done in LA.

Q. If I'm in the market for a complete suspension, either front or rear, what should I look for, how can I tell which is the best system to buy?

A. A fellow can come in the shop, any shop, and generally he can see good workmanship. If the shop is orderly and neat it's more likely that the work will reflect that. Most of our *customers are referrals.*

Q. Your business has grown a lot over the years, how big do you see Kugel Komponents becoming?

A. I prefer to stay small. I don't want 30 employees, I'm happy with the size we are, that way I can keep an eye on things.

Q. The independent rear-end assemblies are a more recent product for you. Can you describe them and how you came to manufacture those as well?

A. We were using Jag rear ends, installing them in street rods. But they were getting harder and harder to find, and when we got one, it was in terrible shape. I knew it would come to a point where I had to step up to building my own independent rear suspension. I took a lot of the points from a Jag, how the lower control arms are affixed and the way they use the half shafts as suspension components. The Corvette suspension is similar.

I tried to make it easy to build and install. It's easier to put the rear end in than the front, and that helps the builders and dealers. It was necessity. We use a 9-inch Ford third-member, we cast up a housing and have that heat treated. Currie makes our axles, either with 31 or 28 splines. We use Corvette calipers mounted inboard and our own custom rotors. The lower arms are investment cast stainless steel or round tube. We use a Corvette hub bearing pack, the upright is our own, made from cast aluminum. The halfshafts are variable in length. On heavier cars we use two coil-overs per side; it makes for a really nice ride. On the lighter cars we only use one coil-over per side. The lower arm is designed so it can be cut off to match the length of the half shaft. Our normal range in width is from 54 to 62 inches, hub to hub.

Q. What are the advantages of using an independent suspension in the rear of the car?

A. Ride quality and handling. With independent on the front and rear, the cars ride better—there is no comparison. With a typical hot rod going down the road, you bounce as you go over bumps and railroad tracks. With an independent suspension you have less unsprung weight, and they ride so much better. Plus they look great and can be tailored to any application.

Q. When a person buys or installs a complete suspension system, what should he or she look out for?

A. All of our products are built to perfection. The installer has the brunt of the responsibility. I've seen supposedly good installers screw up the installation. Choose the builder with care—there are good ones and not so good ones. Competition has kept it good, the bad shops get weeded out. SEMA helps to police the industry too.

Q. Any final words of wisdom?

A. I'm real fortunate to have a job I like—on weekends when I don't come to the shop I get a little bored. I also have two great kids who help me run the shop; they're an enormous amount of help to me. I'd have to say I'm pretty lucky.

Chapter 5

Shocks and Springs

The hot rod world uses at least three types of springs and two types of shock absorbers. Though shocks and springs might seem simple, they are in fact complex and certainly important enough to warrant a separate chapter.

First, let's start with a spring that supports a weight. If you compress the spring and let go, it doesn't just bounce back to the starting point. No, it goes well past that point before reversing direction and going through a series of diminishing oscillations which eventually bring it back to the starting point.

If we are describing the spring that supports one corner of your hot rod, the-up-and down motion makes it difficult to keep the car under control.

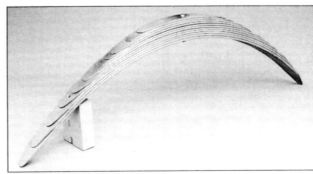

This spring pack is specifically manufactured to work with the 1940-Ford-style rear main leaf and provide a good ride and the correct ride height on a 1932 Ford. *SO-CAL*

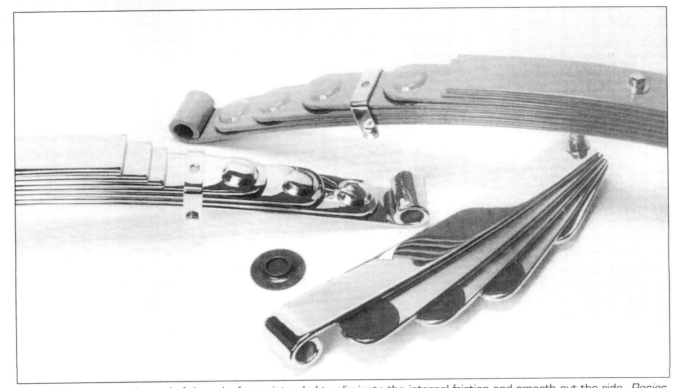

The buttons seen on the end of these leafs are intended to eliminate the internal friction and smooth out the ride. *Posies*

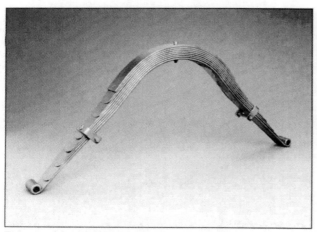

This narrowed Model A rear spring is intended to be used with the Model A–style quick-change cross-member. *SO-CAL*

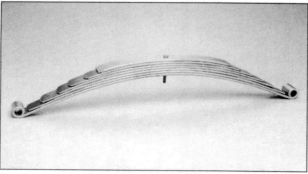

The front spring needs to be matched to both the weight of the car and the specific front axle being used. This example from SO-CAL, designed to work with 1932 Fords, is available in three distinct versions. *SO-CAL*

To dampen those oscillations, a shock absorber is used to prevent the spring from going through the whole series of uncontrolled oscillations.

What's a Spring?

Springs are classified by their rate, that is, how far they move when supporting a certain weight. The spring that's part of a hot rod coil-over might be rated at 200 pounds per inch, meaning that 200 pounds will compress the spring 1 inch. Most coil springs are linear in their rate: if 200 pounds compresses the spring 1 inch, 400 will displace it 2 *inches* (obviously this will change as a coil spring approaches coil bind).

A variable-rate spring provides a progressive rate. By winding the coils more tightly at one end (or by decreasing the diameter of the wire) the engineer is able to create a spring with a soft rate for the first inch or two of travel, and a stiffer rate for the final two inches of travel. If you think about it, a typical leaf spring with five or more leafs is a variable-rate spring. A soft bump will cause only the long main leaf to deflect slightly while a big pot hole might deflect all the leaves in the pack.

What we call leaf springs should be described technically as semi-elliptical leaf springs. Full-elliptic springs are seen on some early cars and consist of two sets of leaves acting against each other. The two sets form a full ellipse. Most of these consist of a pack of flattened "leaves." The main leaf has an eye at either end; these eyes attach to the frame, with a bushing at one end and a shackle at the other. Both Detroit and the hot rod aftermarket manufacture leaf springs that consist of only one leaf, with no pack of smaller leafs.

Leaf springs have been very popular from the earliest days of the automobile and were in fact used to soften the ride on great granddad's buggy. Part of the allure of leaf springs, especially in the early days of automobiles, is the relative ease with which one can be built. Even the local blacksmith can hammer one out from a piece of heated steel and then give it temper with a dip in the vat of cooling water. Leaf springs have a second advantage: they locate the axles or suspension members, thereby simplifying the construction of early automobiles.

The downside to a leaf spring includes a certain minimal sex appeal. Besides that, leaf springs are heavier for a given capacity than a coil spring. However, they compensate for some of that weight gain by eliminating one or more suspension arms.

When I spoke with Ken Fenical, owner of Posies and perhaps the best-known manufacturer of hot rod springs, he was excited about quarter elliptic springs. Essentially, these applications take what we call a leaf spring and cut it in half. Seen recently on the front of some nifty track-roadster-type hot rods, the quarter elliptic bolts the thickest part of the spring pack to the frame and then attaches the end of the main leaf to the axle.

Coil springs take their name from the shape of the spring. Both the coil spring used on the front of a Mustang II type of suspension and the spring used to wrap a modern coil-over are coil springs, yet they display different properties, which we will consider shortly.

As mentioned, coil springs are rated in weight per distance (lb/in in the United States). The simplest springs are linear in their strength. Some springs are said to be "progressive," meaning the coils are wound tighter on one end than the other. Some manufacturers offer a dual-rate spring made up of two different springs stacked on top of each other. Small bumps compress both springs, which provides a softer effective rate. When the softer spring coil binds, then the rate of the stiffer spring kicks in.

Buying Springs

Buying leaf springs is pretty much a matter of matching your needs to the growing number of spring options in the catalog. These springs are typically listed by the application, not by their rate.

In terms of strength and how high from the ground a particular spring will put your car, the best advice comes from the individual manufacturer. Many of the springs are available in standard form or de-arched to help get the car low and minimize the need for lowering blocks.

De-arching is an option for any leaf spring (and a better idea than removing individual leafs). You need to decide how much lower you want the

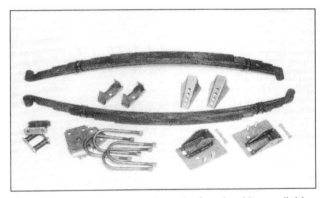

For the bow-tie fan come these leaf spring kits available for most 1932 to 1948 Chevrolets. *Posies*

car and give that specification to the boys at the spring shop. Before proceeding, consider that de-arching effectively makes the spring longer and can create an unusual shackle angle. In some cases the upper shackle pivot may have to be moved back an inch or two.

If your street rod runs coil springs at one or both ends, then the options for spring choice are a little different. In the case of a Mustang-type suspension, the springs are usually ordered at the time you buy the suspension kit. If the springs come from the junkyard or swap meet, remember that not all Mustang IIs or Pintos came with the same springs. Later cars and cars with air conditioning or the V-6 engine used heavier springs. The best recommendation for spring strength in these cases can probably be had from the manufacturer of the suspension kit.

When you go looking for coil springs in the junkyard, remember the formula for coil-spring stiffness. Stiffness = Diameter of the spring wire (W) taken to the fourth power, times a constant (G, the shear modulus for spring steel), divided by 8 times the number of active coils (N), times the diameter of the spring (D) taken to the third power. Written it looks like this:

$$\text{Stiffness} = W^4 \times G / 8 \times N \times D^3$$

Note that very small increases in the diameter of the coil wire make large changes in spring stiffness. Second, by cutting the number of coils you make a coil spring stiffer, not softer (the number of

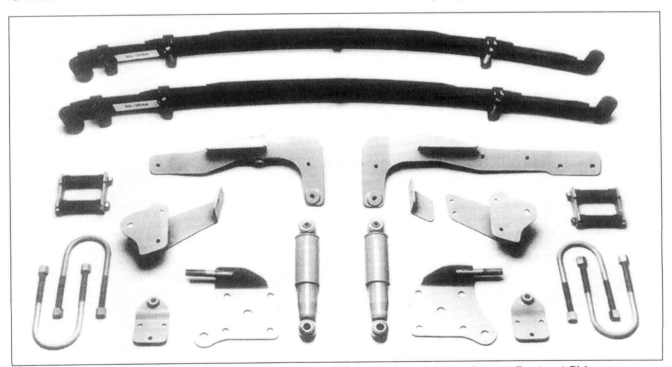

Complete leaf spring kits designed to provide a nice low ride height are available to fit most Ford and GM cars. *Chassis Engineering*

Ken Fenical, known to most people in the industry as Posies, has been manufacturing springs for more than 25 years.

Ken Fenical, owner of Posies, is well known as the builder of street rods that expand the envelope in a design sense. He is also the best-known manufacturer of springs and spring kits for hot rods. With over 30 years of experience, Ken is a man with some sound advice for anyone who's puzzled by the many different springs on the market today.

Q: Ken, give us some background on you and the company.

A: Posies is a name that I took off my father's flower shop building.

When I was a kid my nickname was Posies, and when I got my old 1930 Model A panel truck I put the name on the side. Later I cut a flower outline and the letters from a piece of steel and put them on my father's building. Then when he died I took that sign and put it on my own building, because by then I was ready to open my own business. That was in 1964. I've always had an interest *in cars,* even when I was younger. When I was a kid if something broke Dad would buy me the

tools to fix it, rather than giving me the money to pay someone else to do the repair.

Q: How did you happen to focus on springs and suspensions?

A: Well, I was already having springs manufactured for my customers' cars. Then in 1975 I had 30 springs made to fit the Super Bell dropped axle. I took those to the regional Nationals in Maryland. Joe Mayall from *StreetScene* magazine took a picture of the spring and ran it as a new product release and that's really where it started. I promised Jim Ewing from Super Bell that if he brought out more axles, I would make springs to fit them.

Q: How did you come up with the buttons on the end of each leaf?

A: I started doing that as early as 1963, as a way to eliminate the friction between the leafs. We kind of picked our own trade name, moly nylon, for the buttons. They work good and they've been well accepted in the industry.

Q: When people talk about springs, they talk about a "Hollywood Roll." What is a Hollywood Roll?

A: When a spring leaf comes out of the furnace it goes through a set of rollers. And if it's done properly the leaf will mushroom and thin out toward the end of each leaf. That's the way the Hollywood Spring shop made the springs in the 1940s and that's where the name comes from. Those last 3 or 4 inches of spring are real important, it's what gives it the right deflection properties.

Q: Suppose I'm building a hot rod with a dropped front axle. How do I pick the right front spring for my axle?

A. We have 12 springs for all the combinations of axles on the marketplace today, and they come in three different heights: stock eye, reversed eye, and reversed eye low spring. I should note that the frame may need to be notched for spring clearance on most '28 through '34 cars when using the lowest spring.

If you call us, we will ask you which brand of axle you have and what is the perch distance. On '28 through '48 cars, we also ask what is your kingpin distance and the wheel width—this is just so we know you aren't going to have tire-to-fender clearance problems. If you call and say it's a '32, we need to know if the frame has a Model A crossmember, like the SO-CAL chassis does, because that will help to lower the car. And we also need to know if the car is a coupe/roadster or a sedan, so we can determine how heavy it is.

Q: For rear suspension, what are some of the advantages and disadvantages of a buggy versus parallel leaf springs? And how do coil-overs compare to leaf springs?

A: There are no disadvantages to a buggy spring versus parallel leafs. They ride the same. It's more a matter of whether people want that traditional suspension, and which is easier to install. In fact our newest spring is a Hollywood Roll–type of buggy spring with hidden buttons so it looks really traditional.

When it comes to parallel leafs versus coil-overs, the parallels out-ride the coils, hands down. We sell both, but I've had plenty of customers take out the coil-overs and install leafs. It's hard to beat the ride of a multipack leaf spring. However, the very best riding spring in my opinion is large-diameter coils, but street rodders don't run them.

Q: What kind of mistakes do people make in buying springs and suspension for their hot rods?

A: They run the pressure recommended by the tire manufacturer in radial tires, which means they're too hard for a street rod, which is a lot lighter than a typical sedan. The result is a stiff sidewall and a harsh ride.

Sometimes they've put a bind on the front spring trying to achieve enough caster on a raked frame with a stock cross-member. Obviously the spring won't move like it should and the ride is terrible. In those cases they can put in one of our adjustable spring perches, which allows for enough adjustment without binding the spring.

Or they're simply running an old spring, and it's stiff because of the embrittlement that takes place over time. They need a new spring. Those are just a few of the things we see.

Built from billet aluminum, this Viper coil-over is meant for street rod applications. Available for front or rear, the Viper has adjustable valving for rebound damping. *Pete and Jake's*

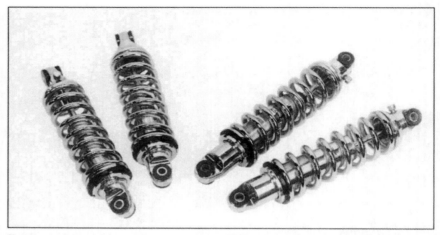

Polished shock bodies and chrome-plated springs make for a good-looking coil-over, especially important when the suspension is highly visible. Like most high-quality shocks, these are available with a variety of springs and offer a six-position adjustment for rebound damping. *Heidt's*

coils is on the bottom of the formula). Third, small changes in the diameter of the spring itself result in relatively large increases in stiffness. As the spring gets bigger in diameter, it also gets softer.

At this point we have to insert a warning label concerning coil springs: A compressed coil spring stores an enormous amount of energy.

Coil springs have the capacity to kill and maim. If you aren't familiar with the removal and installation of coil springs, ask for help or truck the whole thing down to the local suspension or front-end shop.

Experienced builders advise owners that it's better to go too soft than too hard when choosing springs. Most manufacturers offer technical assistance in the choice of both springs and shocks for your car. Note that a constant-rate coil spring should never bottom out, or "coil bind." When you bottom out the coil it stresses the metal and causes fatigue. Be sure the coil springs aren't too long for the job and that the axle hits the snubber before either the shock or coil spring reach the end of their travel.

Before buying coil-overs for your car, consider the mounting angle of the shock and spring assembly. As the coil-over moves from vertical to horizontal, the effective strength of the spring is reduced. At a 20-degree lean, for example, the effective spring rate is only 88 percent of the original rating. So, if your coil-overs are mounted at a 20-degree angle from vertical, you need to use a 227 lb/in spring to get a true 200 lb/in spring rate.

Some of the charts mentioned earlier are already corrected for lean; if not, you have to use the correction factor to arrive at the correct spring rate.

The manufacturer of the spring for your coil-over may offer to exchange them if they turn out to be too stiff or too soft—it's something worth

considering when looking at two competing brands of coil-overs.

New to hot rods is the air spring, a concept that OEM auto and truck manufacturers have used for some time. Air springs come to the party with a number of inherent advantages. One is light weight, another is the air spring's progressive nature.

The formula for an air spring reads as follows: $F = pa$, where F is the force applied to the spring strut, p is the air pressure, and a is the area of the piston. Assuming there is no temperature change in the air and that the bag or air spring does not deflect (which would change the volume), when you cut the area in half you double the pressure. In the real world there probably is some bag deflection and some temperature change, yet for all intents and purposes the air spring offers the hot rodder a spring with a progressive rate without the need for sophisticated linkages or specially wound coils.

Shock Absorbers

Damper is the correct term to use when describing the hydraulic device that dampens the oscillations of a spring. Like leaf springs, shock absorbers have been used since the earliest days of the automobile. The first shocks were friction shocks. As the name suggests, these early shocks worked by rubbing a series of discs *together* to dampen the up-and-down movement of the springs. The problem is the tendency of these early shocks to exert their greatest resistance at the beginning of movement. Once the initial "stiction" is overcome, a friction shock offers reduced resistance to movement. This is pretty much the opposite of what an engineer looks for in a shock absorber. Ever the innovator, Henry Ford was one of the first to

A complete air-suspension system requires more than just an air bag at each corner. In addition to the control panel, the system includes an air compressor, reservoir tank, and all the lines and fittings.

understand the importance of shock absorbers, even on an inexpensive car, when he specified hydraulic lever shocks for the new Model A.

Today, tubular hydraulic shocks are virtually the only type used, and many of these use gas charging (more later) to improve the characteristics of a standard hydraulic shock absorber.

Unsprung Weight and Shock Absorbers

At this point we need to digress and discuss sprung and unsprung weight, terms you're likely to see if you pick up a book or article about suspension design for cars. It's also a factor you should consider when trying to decide which shocks, brakes, and wheels to buy. Most of the car—the frame, engine, and body—is considered sprung weight, that is, weight supported by and acting on the springs. The wheels, tires, and brake components on the other hand are considered unsprung weight.

Consider your car as it goes down the road and hits a sharp bump. The bump forces the wheel up, compressing the spring. One of the goals of any good suspension system is to keep the tires on the pavement. When the bump in question drops away

quickly you want the wheel to change direction rapidly and stay in contact with the asphalt.

The problem at this point is the momentum of the wheel and tire, which makes them want to continue moving in an upward direction even after the pavement falls away. The compressed spring is trying to force apart the wheel and the frame. How much of the spring's energy raises the car and how much of it forces the tire down depends on the ratio of sprung to unsprung weight.

A lighter wheel/tire/brake assembly will react more quickly to irregularities in the road while at the same time feeding less energy into the rest of the chassis. The compression damping of the shock absorber controls the sprung weight of the car, or how fast the spring is compressed as you hit a certain bump at a certain speed. The rebound damping, however, controls the movement of the unsprung weight—the wheel, tire, and hub assembly—as they change direction and move away from the car.

Henry's early shocks were lever-action hydraulic shocks, though today most cars are equipped with tubular shocks. Simply put, tubular shocks have a piston inside that pushes oil through internal valves and passages as the shock is compressed and extended. By changing the internal valving and oil viscosity in a shock, manufacturers can alter the rate of compression and rebound to suit a particular vehicle. A Detroit sedan might come with shocks that are much softer on compression than they are on rebound—done as a means of achieving a good compromise between ride and suspension control. Hot rod shock absorbers tend to be valved closer to 50/50 (the same on compression and rebound).

The more sophisticated shocks use valves that respond to speed and inertia. A sharp bump encountered at relatively high speed compresses the shock very quickly. A high-quality shock senses this speed of movement and unseats a large orifice so the shock is effectively softer in this situation. The same shock will open a smaller orifice for a smaller bump, essentially creating a shock that automatically changes its rate from soft to firm.

Buy the Good Stuff

Fluid friction provides the damping in a modern shock absorber. A shock that works too hard, however, will heat up as the result of that friction. Cheap shocks allow air to mix with the oil, and the oil itself to change viscosity due to the heat. Either situation results in poor and inconsistent damping as the piston moves through an aerated froth of hot oil.

Inconsistent damping control and aerated oil are problems overcome by high-quality shock absorbers. In a quality shock absorber, all the components, from pistons to shafts, are larger and built to higher standards. The valves that control the damping are much more sophisticated to better handle a variety of road conditions and driving styles. To better handle the heat, the amount of oil is increased. For better cooling, the body of the shock can be made of aluminum. To prevent aeration of the oil, the shock is gas-charged, or filled with a premium oil that won't change viscosity.

Mounting Tips

Though it sounds too obvious to mention, experienced builders say they often see cars where the upper and lower shock mounting pins (on a double-eye design) aren't parallel. Though most of these eyes are lined with rubber, the rubber bushings will only compensate for minor misalignment. Serious misalignment can cause the shock to wear out prematurely, bind, or even break the mount.

We've stated more than once the fact that shocks aren't meant to take the place of the rubber suspension snubbers. Though it's generally alright for the shock to limit the suspension travel in extension, you don't want the shock to be the limiting factor on compression. Like all rules, this one has an

exception. That exception is the shocks, mainly coilovers, that come with a small synthetic donut located on the shaft just under the head (see the photo). These cushions are made from some high-tech material developed by firms like Koni to take the place of the external rubber and synthetic snubbers seen on most OEM applications. In some cases the size and design of the built-in snubber can be changed.

Speaking of snubbers, Jim Sleeper from SO-CAL points out that in cars with very limited suspension travel, the snubber effectively acts as another spring. If your car routinely hits the suspension stops, and those are hard enough to "bounce the car up into the air" you're going to have a car that's very hard to handle.

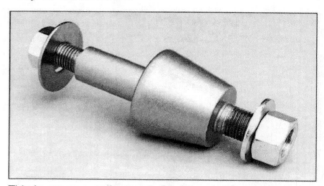

This lower rear coil-over stud is intended to space the shock far enough away from the housing that the spring won't rub on the rear end. *SO-CAL*

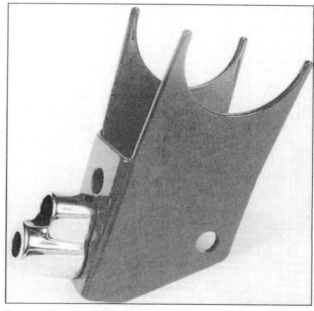

This lower coil-over bracket comes with three mounting holes for height adjustment. The spacer moves the coilover away from the rear end and also spreads the load to two mounting holes instead of just one. *Deuce Factory*

In a large shop like the one at SO-CAL, each person has their specialty. Some are welders and some are fabricators. Jim Sleeper might be called the resident chassis expert. Jim says he got into the chassis business by accident. "I had a '68 Camaro and after I did a curb shot I had to fix the car myself."

From fixing Camaros, Jim went on to automotive classes at Fullerton College and then to a big alignment shop. More recently Jim worked with companies like Bell Tech and Koni in the design of suspension components for lowered trucks. And before that he did chassis setup for competition cars, both for drag racing and SCCA. Today, Jim is a man who can handle a front-end alignment in the morning and then use the CAD/CAM software on the computer in the afternoon.

Street rods ask a lot of their suspension components. With limited travel and very simple suspension designs, making a street rod ride and handle can be a challenge. Jim Sleeper is a man with answers to questions that most of us are asking.

If you ask Jim how to pick the shocks for any given street rod, he backs up right away and wants to talk about the suspension. "What street rodders need in a shock is first to figure out the amount of travel in the suspension. They need enough up-and-down travel for the suspension to work. Once they have enough travel and they have the right spring, then they need to find the right shock—the shock is what controls the suspension.

"The shock needs to be the right length, so it doesn't bottom. It needs enough rebound damping to control the spring. Compression is important but rebound is more important—it needs enough damping on rebound to control the suspension. Shocks with a single damping adjustment are letting the owner control the rebound damping, so people who have those shocks need to understand the shock and get them adjusted correctly."

The limited amount of travel allowed by many of these suspensions makes it hard for any spring/shock combination to work correctly. "The suspension runs *into* the bump stop all the time," explains Jim, "and then the car gets shot up into the air. No shock can control that." Of course, some builders avoid the problem by ignoring the need for a bump stop, which greatly shortens the life of the shock absorber.

Despite the advice of some shock manufacturers, Jim likes his shocks close to vertical. "Shocks need to be as straight up as possible and as close to the wheel as they can be. The shock is the control part of the suspension; you have better leverage closer to the tire. If you mount them at an angle, then you need to pay attention to the compensation table that most shock manufacturers provide."

The discussion of shock mounting brought up the subject of coil-overs and how the springs should be chosen. Jim's approach is very straightforward. For a hot rod with a solid rear axle, he starts by weighing the back of the car, then subtracting from that figure the unsprung weight—the weight of the axle, wheels, tires, brakes, and half the shocks and springs. Now he divides that weight by 2. Next he divides that figure by the number of inches of compression travel in the suspension. Now, he factors in the position of the coil-over relative to the wheel. If the distance from the center of the car to the wheel is 20 inches and the shock is mounted at 15 inches, then it's 3/4 of the way out to the tire so you divide by .75 to arrive at the basic spring rate.

So far Jim's example goes like this (all numbers are rounded to the closest whole number): 1,000 pounds/2 = 500. 500/5 (inches of compression travel) = 100 pounds per inch.

100/.75 = 133; that's the rate you need for the spring half of the vertical coil-over. If the coil-over is mounted at a 30-degree angle, then you need to compensate for the angle with the correction factor. The correction factor for a 30-degree lean is .75. We need a stronger spring to compensate for the lean angle of the coil-over so we divide the original number, 133, by .75 = 178 pounds per inch.

Enough math. If you ask Jim where hot rodders and street rodders make their suspension mistakes, he thinks it's by talking to the wrong people: "People who don't really know what they're talking about when it comes to suspensions." His other advice involves the quality of the suspension components that people buy: "The components should come from well-known manufacturers. And street rodders often don't allow for enough suspension travel. Sometimes they make it worse by limiting even that travel, by binding the front spring on a buggy spring setup, for example.

"People forget how important the tires are. You have such a small patch of rubber holding such enormous weight—they should check the tire pressures more often and take care that the alignment is correct. And the car should be built so that if all four tires go flat, nothing hits the ground, not the oil pan or one corner of the frame or a lower shock mount—that's the most important safety rule there is.

93

Chapter 6

Brakes

People are always talking about the "good old days." Well, things weren't always better back then. At least not for hot rodders. First, there weren't nearly as many components and kits available for the first-time builder. Second, some of the kits and components that were available left a lot to be desired.

Case in point is the early Mustang II front suspension often used by street rodders looking for independent suspension. While the suspension itself usually worked fine, many of those kits and clips came with the factory Mustang II brakes. The result was a hot rod with 9-inch rotors and a single-piston factory caliper.

If the car in question was a nice light coupe, everything worked just fine. On the other hand, if the car in question was a fat-fendered sedan with a big-block, air conditioning, and a small trailer out behind, well, that's another story.

You'll notice that all the current ads for brakes in the hot rod and street rod press talk about how their system uses some derivative of the Mustang II suspension, but one that's upgraded with "vented 11-inch rotors and a midsize GM (or something similar) caliper." Nearly everyone has learned their basic physics: brakes that work on a 2,000-pound highboy can't stop a car that's nearly twice as heavy, especially at high speed.

What are called "big Mustang II" kits are not all the same. This example uses 11 inch vented rotors and full-size (not metric) GM calipers, along with all necessary brackets and aluminum hubs. Unlike some, this kit does not move the wheels outboard. *ECI*

Pete and Jake's offers another front brake kit with four-piston Wilwood aluminum calipers and vented rotors. When ordering aluminum calipers, it's a good idea to order them with stainless steel pistons. *Pete and Jake's*

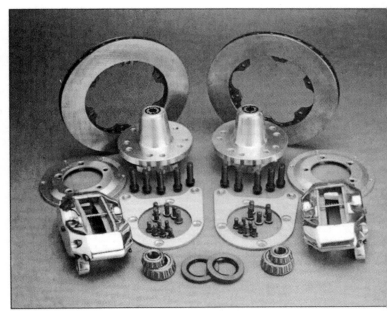

Designed to fit 1937 to 1948 Ford spindles, this kit uses an aluminum hub with 0.812-inch vented rotors, caliper brackets, and Wilwood four-piston aluminum calipers. *TCI*

Vented rotors handle the heat of stopping better due to the fact that the vents help them cool, and they have more total mass. These vented rotors are designed to replace the solid rotors that came with many Mustang IIs and Pintos. They use stock bearings and come in a variety of five-bolt patterns. *Heidt's*

The textbooks talk about kinetic (moving) energy and explain the basic relationship between kinetic energy, mass, and speed. Another formula: kinetic energy = $1/2 MV^2$. So, your car's kinetic energy equals half its weight multiplied by the speed squared. When you double the weight you double the kinetic energy. Increasing the speed makes a nonlinear change in energy, however. Doubling the speed produces four times the kinetic energy (all other factors being equal). Of course energy can't be created or destroyed, only converted to another form—in this case, heat. Thus, when you stomp on the brake pedal at 80 miles per hour, you are converting four times the kinetic energy into heat than you are at 40 miles per hour.

What all this really means is that the little, nonvented, wimpy rotors from an American econo-box just aren't going to do the job for your 1940 Ford sedan. You need bigger rotors and bigger calipers that can dissipate the heat. After all, these are hot rods.

The bigger *rotors that* now come standard with many brake kits work to your advantage in at least three ways: First, the larger diameter gives the caliper more leverage. Second, larger rotors allow you to use larger calipers. These come with bigger pads that are better able to grab hold of the spinning rotors. Finally, the larger components, both rotors and calipers, are better able to absorb the heat simply because of their increased surface area (especially with vented rotors) and mass. The other bit of physics that we should slip in here is the fact, probably well known, that the front

brakes do at least 70 percent of the stopping on a hard brake application.

So, unless there are overriding aesthetic considerations, the front brakes should be discs. They're self-cleaning, they cool faster than drum brakes, and they also provide more total braking power for a given amount of weight than do drum brakes.

Like many Detroit manufacturers, you may want to use discs in front *and drums in the rear.* In that case what you want is more than just raw

Designed to fit 1938 to 1948 Ford spindles, this front brake kit from Magnum Axle utilizes an aluminum hub, vented rotor, caliper, and bracket. *SO-CAL*

What appears to be a Buick finned brake drum is really a simple cover. Underneath are the real brake components: a Wilwood four-piston caliper squeezing a vented rotor mounted to an aluminum hub. *SO-CAL*

stopping power. You want balance in the total system (more later). Whether it's a disc/drum system or pure discs, you need brakes big enough to handle the weight of your car, with front and rear components that are compatible, and a master cylinder with a bore diameter of the right size to apply both the front and rear bakes.

The discussion of disc versus drum brakes brings up the new disc brake system, designed by Paul Carrol and sold by the SO-CAL Speed Shop. A perfect combination of form and function, the SO-CAL "finned Buick brakes" use a Wilwood two-piston aluminum caliper and 11-inch vented rotor to provide good, modern stopping power. With a backing plate styled after an early Ford and a cover that looks exactly like a Buick brake drum, the whole affair comes off looking like a very traditional set of drum brakes.

To match the Buick "drums" used on the front, SO-CAL has recently announced a new Buick drum for the rear. This new rear brake drum is actually a cover that slides over the rear drums used on a typical Ford 9-inch rear end. When viewed from the back, these new covers look exactly like a finned Buick brake drum.

How Your Brakes Work

When you step on the brake pedal, you displace hydraulic fluid from the master cylinder and create hydraulic pressure in the system. Because the brake fluid is a non-compressible liquid, the pressure created at the outlet to the master cylinder is applied fully to the pistons in the calipers or wheel cylinders. None of this pressure is "used up" compressing the fluid link between the master cylinder and the calipers. When you're buying or installing the brakes on your hot rod, it's a good idea to keep in mind the two laws that govern hydraulic behavior: Pressure in the brake system is equal over all surfaces of the system, and a fluid cannot be compressed to a smaller volume.

The problem with all this hydraulic business is the fact that we need more than pressure, we also need volume. This brings up the fascinating subject of hydraulic ratios.

A demonstration might help explain the need to match the master cylinder with the calipers or wheel cylinders. The pressure of the hydraulic fluid at the master cylinder outlet is determined by that old formula from high school: Pressure = Force/Area. If you put 10 pounds of force on the master cylinder piston with 1 square inch of area, you have created a pressure of 10 psi. If you apply the same amount, 10 pounds, of force to a master cylinder with only 1/2 square inch of piston area, then you've created twice the pressure, 20 psi.

Remember that the full pressure created at the master cylinder outlet is available to apply to either calipers or wheel cylinder pistons. So if we apply that 10 psi of pressure to the caliper with 1 square inch of piston area, the force on the brake pad will be 10 pounds (Force = Pressure x Area). Now, if you double the piston area you also double the force on the brake pad. *Thus, the way to achieve* maximum force on the brake pads is with a small master cylinder piston connected to calipers with large or multiple pistons and a large total area.

Now you get smart and decide to eliminate any need for a power booster by using a master cylinder with a small-diameter piston. There is, as always, a trade-off here. The smaller piston doesn't move as much fluid as a larger one, and the pedal may be right on the floor when you've finally moved it far enough to displace enough fluid to push the pads against the rotor.

This brings you to the realization that what's needed here is a good balance between the master cylinder and the calipers or wheel cylinders. You can't just go to smaller and smaller diameter master cylinder pistons or bigger and bigger caliper pistons. In the real world you probably want more pressure, but still need a master cylinder piston big enough to displace a certain volume of fluid.

Most experienced hot rod builders suggest you build the right system the first time, without relying on a power booster to overcome deficiencies in the design of the overall brake system.

You need to design the system around a good manual master cylinder and then consider the ideal balance between front and rear brakes (whether it's four-wheel discs or not) and how that balance is achieved. Detroit uses a combination valve between the front and rear brakes to help balance out a disc/drum brake system. That combination valve does more than "balance" the brakes; in most cases it helps the system overcome two little problems with a split, disc/drum brake system.

The first little fly in the ointment when building a combination system is that drum brakes require more pressure for their initial application than do disc brakes. Drum brakes, with their big shoes, return springs, and relatively large distance between the shoes and the drum, require approximately 125 psi to actually push the shoes against the drums with enough force to slow down the car. Disc brakes, however, need only about one-tenth as much pressure to push the pads against the rotor with enough force to affect the car's speed.

The first job then of the factory combination valve is to "hold off" the front brakes until the system reaches approximately 125 psi. In this way the car uses both the front and rear brakes to do the stopping, even on a light pedal application.

Job two for the combination valve is to slow the pressure rise to the rear brakes on a hard brake application. Consider that on an easy stop from slow speed, there is little weight transfer and the rear tires maintain good traction. Now, consider the same car stopping hard from high speed. In this case there is a great deal of weight transfer onto the front tires. This leaves the rear tires with little bite and in danger of locking up. In this situation the proportioning function in the combination

In a split disc/drum system, it's important that the rear brakes apply first. This hold-off/metering valve will delay the application of the front brakes. *ECI*

valve limits the rate at which the line pressure is applied to the rear brakes in order to prevent the rear tires from locking up.

Many professional builders, SO-CAL among them, don't use a combination valve simply because, as Shane explains, "We've never found one that's designed for a hot rod." Instead they rely on the often-seen adjustable proportioning valve to limit the pressure delivered to the rear brakes.

Using Residual Pressure Valves

A fair amount of confusion surrounds the use of residual pressure valves in a brake system. Drum and disc brakes have very different needs here, and even all the disc systems don't have the same requirements.

A drum brake system, any drum brake system, needs a 10- to 12-pound residual-pressure check valve in the hydraulic system. On OEM applications, this valve is usually built into the master cylinder. As the name suggests, these valves maintain a small amount of pressure on the drum brakes at all times; this pressure keeps the lips of the cups expanded out against the wheel cylinder bore. This prevents air ingestion past the wheel cylinder cups when you release the brake pedal. This means that when you buy a master cylinder, you need to buy one with the correct bore diameter, and match it to the type of brakes, disc or drum, used on either end of your new car.

The use of that same 10-pound residual check valve on a disc brake system *will* create brake drag, quickly ruining the pads and rotors. You

Inline residual pressure valves come in 2 and 10 pound ratings. The 2-pound valve is needed in a disc brake system when the calipers are higher than the master. The 10-pound valve is needed in drum brake applications when the valve is not built into the master cylinder. *ECI*

need a check valve on a disc brake system *only* when the master cylinder is mounted lower than the calipers. In this case, a *2-pound* check valve prevents the fluid in the caliper from siphoning back to the master cylinder.

Brake Fluid

You might think brake fluid is just that, brake fluid. However, the shelves at the auto parts store carry at least three separate grades of brake fluid, which is essentially a very specialized hydraulic fluid designed to operate in a potentially dirty environment under a wide range of temperatures. Obviously the fluid must stay viscous at below-zero temperatures, and yet resist boiling at the very high temperatures brake components are often subjected to. If the brake fluid boils, it becomes a gas and thus a compressible material, resulting in a spongy brake pedal.

The three grades of brake fluid commonly available are DOT 3, DOT 4, and DOT 5. DOT 3 and 4 are glycol-based fluids with dry boiling points of 401 and 446 degrees Fahrenheit respectively. Either fluid is suitable for use in disc brake systems. There are two basic problems with DOT 3 and DOT 4 brake fluids: they tend to absorb water from the environment (they are hygroscopic) and they attack most painted surfaces.

Glycol-based brake fluid containers must be kept closed so the fluid won't pick up moisture from the air. Because the DOT 3 or 4 brake fluid in your car will pick up some water no matter how careful you are, it's a good idea to flush the system with fresh fluid every couple of years. Remember that brake fluid contaminated with water boils at a much lower temperature and can be corrosive to components.

DOT 5 fluid is silicone based and has a higher boiling point of 500 degrees Fahrenheit, dry. This more expensive fluid doesn't absorb water and doesn't react with paint (though silicone fluid can stain paint if not washed off quickly).

Like every other advance, silicone brake fluid has its trade-offs. As mentioned, silicone fluid costs more, it is slightly compressible, it aerates more easily than glycol-based fluid, and it is said to cause swelling of the brake cups and seals after long-term exposure. Some brake-component manufacturers don't recommend the use of silicone fluid, so be sure to check before filling the master cylinder. And once you have filled the master cylinder, don't switch from one type of brake fluid to another—they're not compatible.

The Purchasing Decision

Before buying, consider that job number one is stopping and slowing the car during street driving (remember these are *street* rods). These may be hot rods, but they are not race cars. Though the race car stuff may look impressive, it doesn't always work better than—or even as well as—components and systems designed for street use, and that includes good old OEM stuff from Detroit.

What you buy will depend on your budget and intended use, as well as the car's weight, bolt pattern, spindle, and style. In general you want to buy as much brake as you can for a given amount of cash. An engineer once explained to me: "When you're considering brakes, more is usually better. More surface area, more pistons, and larger calipers."

Given the fact that the front brakes do 70 percent (or more) of the stopping in a hard stop, it makes sense to put your best foot forward. Always put the best brakes on the front.

The high-performance brake assemblies with polished aluminum calipers may look really trick—and most of that equipment works as good as it looks—but that doesn't mean you can't adapt OEM components from Detroit for the front or rear of the new hot rod. You simply have to be sure the parts you use are in good condition (if in doubt buy new or rebuilt components), that they are large enough to deal with your car's weight, and that they are matched to the other components in the brake system.

When considering the rear brakes, it helps to remember that you need more than brakes, you also need a good emergency brake. If you're using stock drum brake assemblies in the rear, you simply need to buy cables and hardware and hook up the stock emergency brakes. If, on the other hand, you're using four-wheel disc brakes, the choice of rear calipers becomes more important because it also determines your emergency brake options.

Rear disc-brake calipers fall into two categories: those with and those without an integral emergency brake. Most of the calipers with an integral emergency brake are from Detroit, though Wilwood now makes a rear brake caliper with an integral emergency brake.

Corvette brake components are turning up on hot rods in increasing numbers, and there's certainly nothing wrong with using them, as long as you keep the system balanced and keep in mind the fact that not all Corvettes used the same brakes.

The calipers used on pre-1984 'Vettes have a host of problems all their own and should probably be avoided entirely. In 1984 the Corvette got a major redesign, and that redesign included new brakes. The new single-piston calipers include a saddle assembly that reinforces the caliper. Some clever hot rodders have removed these saddles as a

For anyone with a 9-inch Ford rear end, this kit offers all-new brake components, including the drum, backing plate, shoes, wheel cylinders, and hardware. *SO-CAL*

If you plan to install disc brakes on the rear, you also need to plan for the emergency brake. These kits include a Cadillac rear caliper with integral emergency brake and vented Trans Am rear rotors. *The kit can be ordered to fit* 8-, 8.8-, and 9-inch Ford rear ends. *ECI*

One answer to the emergency-brake puzzle is to use this small rotor and mechanical caliper on the rearmost U-joint. The only trouble is that the car can still roll off the jack when one rear wheel is jacked up if it's a non-posi rear end. *ECI*

way to make the calipers work with small-diameter wheels. There is such a thing as being too clever, though: these saddles are part of the caliper assembly and should not be removed.

From 1984 to 1988, Corvette rear calipers used a separate emergency brake made up of small shoes that expand against the inside of the rotor. A better choice for the street rodder might be the 1989 and later Corvette rear calipers, which feature a cable-operated emergency brake built into the caliper.

Other cars that use four-wheel discs with an integral rear emergency brake include some Camaros, Toronados, and Eldorados. In the Ford line, certain Lincoln Versailles and even some Granadas used the 9-inch rear end with factory rear disc brakes, and these calipers include integral emergency brakes. However, the latest rear calipers from Ford, used on many Explorers and T-Birds, use a very small-diameter piston and should be avoided.

Aftermarket calipers with no integral emergency brake on the rear axle will force you to come up with your own emergency brake. Some people choose to install an additional rotor mounted at the rear U-joint, clamped by its own mechanical caliper. The potential downside to this is the fact that with a non-limited-slip rear end, if you jack up one wheel, the car can roll off the jack. You can also mount additional, mechanical calipers on the rear rotors, but be sure these are substantial enough to handle emergency and parking duties on a 3,000-pound automobile. In other words, don't use little

Mickey-Mouse mechanical calipers meant for a 300-pound go-cart on your Chevy sedan.

Brake Service

Hot rods tend to be the recipients of maximum TLC during any kind of installation or repair sequences. Yet, when working on the brakes it's essential to go that extra mile to ensure that the brake installation is absolutely bulletproof.

When working on the brakes, it's important to follow the same procedures used by certified mechanics when they do brake work. Start with good attention to detail and follow that up with extreme cleanliness when dealing with the hydraulic system. To bleed brakes, most mechanics start at the bleeder farthest away from the master cylinder (or that half of the master cylinder in a dual-reservoir system). If you've never bled the brakes before, you can get help from a good manual, such as *Motors,* or from the company who sold you the brakes. Another good source of brake service information is the Wilwood Web site (www.wilwood.com), which also includes some very good troubleshooting information.

Perhaps the most important step you perform is the examination of the car's brakes when the work is finished. Pressurize the system with a size 12 sneaker on the brake pedal, then crawl around under the car to check for leakage or seepage from every fitting, caliper, and wheel cylinder.

On a drum brake system, it's important to correctly adjust the brake shoes before adjusting the cables for the emergency brake. Too much tension on the emergency-brake cables or linkage won't allow the shoes to come back against the stop at the top of the backing plate, which makes it impossible to correctly adjust the shoes. So be sure to adjust the brake shoes correctly before you worry about adjusting the cables and linkage for the emergency brake.

Before you're finished with the brakes, do a careful road test. Remember that new brake shoes haven't seated against the drums yet, and that the

A variety of remanufactured calipers, including rear calipers with an integral emergency brake, are available for your hot rod, *as well as the sexier aluminum aftermarket caliper seen on the right. TCI*

hydraulic system might still contain a bit of residual air. In either case, the result can be a soft pedal and reduced braking on the first few applications. So take it easy on the first few stops. Don't be afraid to come back in and re-bleed all or part of the system. Disc brakes don't need adjustment, but the drum brakes, whether self-adjusting or not, need to be adjusted per the recommendations in the service manual.

A few more tips for drum brake assembly: Don't get greasy fingerprints on the new brake shoes. If you do, carefully sand off the greasy spot with some 80-grit sandpaper before slipping on the drum. When installing used components, be sure to have the old drums turned before installation. Have the shop check the drum's finished diameter against the maximum given by the manufacturer to ensure they aren't cut too far. The same applies to disc rotors, which can't be cut past a certain minimal point.

Inactivity is very hard on brake parts. Overhaul or replace wheel cylinders and calipers that come along with the rear end or front calipers you drag out of the junkyard. Discard any old factory rubber hoses and replace them with new components. Master cylinders, too, should be overhauled or simply replaced with new components. Be sure *any* master cylinder you use is a two-chamber design. Solvents will attack the rubber used as seals in brake systems, so all cleaning of hydraulic parts must be done with clean brake fluid.

While not rocket science, caliper overhaul requires a certain finesse. If you've never done it before, take them to the shop down the street or just buy rebuilt assemblies. If you ignore our advice and force the caliper piston from the bore with compressed air, be sure the piston doesn't become an air-powered projectile. Stuff the caliper cavity full of rags first, and be sure to keep your fingers out of the way when applying air to the caliper (ouch). Once apart, pitted caliper pistons need to be replaced, the caliper bore should be thoroughly cleaned with the correct brake hone, and the groove for the main piston seal must be cleaned *thoroughly*. The new seal and the piston should be lubricated with brake fluid or brake-assembly fluid before being installed.

Most of the calipers from Detroit are single-piston designs that float, so the force of a single piston is divided equally between two pads. If the pins or the

Designed for disc brake applications, these chrome-plated, ribbed backing plates mount inside of the rotor and thus add extra sparkle to the front end. *Pete and Jake's*

sliding surfaces are dirty and rusty, the caliper can't float. You must be sure to clean all sliding surfaces, and replace the pins on GM calipers if they're rusty.

Whether the old brakes you're repairing are disc or drum, consider that many of those old pads and shoes contained asbestos. Wear a good respirator or air mask during the disassembly of used brake components, avoid the use of air tools, and don't clean everything up by blowing the "dust" off those old assemblies.

If you've never packed and installed a set of front wheel bearings before, swallow your pride and read a service manual. Plenty of bearings have been ruined because someone was overzealous in tightening the spindle nut, or didn't get enough grease packed between the rollers where it's needed.

When rebuilding the old drum brakes, the hardware and springs that hold and retract the shoes should probably be replaced at the same time you're doing all the other work. Many good automotive parts stores and some street rod vendors sell brake hardware kits for most drum-brake applications.

Caliper brackets should be original or come from a good aftermarket supplier. The full force of a panic stop is transmitted to the chassis through that caliper bracket, so don't skimp. Use a good bracket and bolt it to the spindle assembly with the hardware supplied with the kit or with grade-8 bolts.

Many of the popular front brake kits mentioned earlier for the Mustang II and some early-Ford axles combine an 11-inch ventilated rotor with the

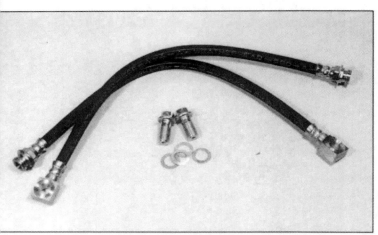

There's nothing wrong with using black, OEM-style flexible hoses for each front wheel and the rear axle. They're DOT approved and readily available in a variety of lengths and styles. *ECI*

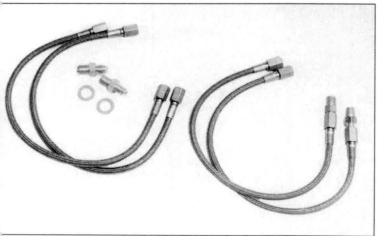

Braided brake lines are available in a variety of lengths and styles. Kits like these can be ordered with the adapters needed to convert from the 37-degree AN fittings to the NPT (National Pipe Thread) or banjo fittings used on many Wilwood or GM calipers. *Heidt's*

intermediate or larger GM caliper. The rotor used in some of these kits is thinner (0.810 inch) than the stock GM rotor (0.960 inch); that's why some of these kits also supply a spacer to be used behind the inner brake pad. If you leave out the spacer, the *piston* comes out farther than the GM engineers intended. This might be all right until the pads become worn, and the end of the piston is pushed past the inner seal and you lose the front brakes.

Nonfloating aftermarket calipers come with a series of small spacers. You will need to use these to center each caliper as it mounts over the rotor. That way each piston moves out of the bore the same distance on a brake application.

When you mount your new or rebuilt caliper to the caliper bracket, you must be sure that the bleeder screw on your new calipers ends up at the top. You have to be sure that the bleeder screw on your new calipers ends up at the top. If not, you will have to bleed the brakes with the calipers off the bracket. Next, hook up the hoses. Hoses should be new and carefully chosen to ensure they are the correct length. It's easy to install a hose that's too short or too long—a hose that will tear on a bump or rub on a tire. During the chassis mock-up, be sure to run the suspension up-and-down, and turn the wheels back and forth to check for any potential clearance problems.

When it comes to flexible hoses, braided lines look great and may be stronger than stock flexible hoses. Most, however, are not DOT approved and could cause your car to be failed during a state inspection (depending on which state you live in).

As for hard lines, a panic stop can generate as much as 1,600 psi in the hydraulic system—too much pressure for anything but an approved steel brake line, with double-flare fittings or systems specifically designed for automotive brakes. See chapter 7 for more on plumbing and fittings approved for brake systems.

Mounting the Master Cylinder and Brake Pedal

Most street rods mount the master cylinder to the frame. This keeps everything mounted low, and all that hardware off the firewall. A variety of mounting brackets are available, or the enterprising builder can fabricate his or her own.

The master cylinder bracket needs to be sturdy, so the full movement of the pedal is transmitted into piston movement and not in flexing the bracket. Many builders mount the bracket solid to the left frame rail and then find a way (easier on some cars than others) to tie the bracket to the X-member or one of the cross-members. While the master cylinder and booster need to be below floor level, you don't want them any lower than necessary.

The dimensions of the pedal assembly determine the pedal ratio, another of those pesky details to be considered when planning the brake system. The pedal ratio is the distance from the pedal to the pivot, divided by the distance from the pivot to the point where the master cylinder pushrod attaches. A high pedal ratio (which means a *long* pedal arm in relation to the pushrod arm) will provide tremendous leverage for your foot, allowing you to generate high line pressure, though the pedal-travel necessary for a given application will increase. Conversely, a low pedal ratio (short pedal arm) will decrease the leverage; meaning an increase in the leg force needed to generate a given amount of pressure and a decrease in the pedal travel. Ralph Lisena from ECI, a manufacturer

Dual chamber master cylinders can be ordered as an assembly, with the under-floor mount and the correct small-diameter power booster. *ECI*

of aftermarket brake kits and components, recommends a ratio of about 4.75 or 5 to 1 as the best for master cylinders with a bore of 7/8 or 1 inch.

As mentioned earlier, it's a good idea to mount the dry master cylinder on the bracket to be sure the pedal can move all the way to the end of its travel without hitting the floor or some other obstruction. Before you do the final installation of the master cylinder, always "bench bleed" it. Fill the reservoir with fluid, then use you fingers as one-way valves, allowing air and fluid to push past your fingertips when the pushrod is moved into the cylinder and sealing the outlets as the pushrod is allowed to come back to its rest position. When you mount the master in the car, the job of bleeding the brakes will go much faster because the master cylinder has already been bled.

If you use a vacuum-operated power brake booster, be sure to install a one-way valve in the vacuum line. Not only will this provide a more constant supply of vacuum to the diaphragm, it will keep gas fumes from flowing from the intake

manifold down the line (remember, they're heavier than air) and into the booster, turning it into a potential bomb.

Be sure the centerline for the pedal pivot is perpendicular to the centerline of the car so the pedal moves straight and not through an arc. Remember that the master usually ends up mounted backwards from the way it was mounted in a Detroit car, so the hoses and reservoirs are backwards. Be absolutely sure it's plumbed correctly, with the front brake reservoir connected to the front brakes. People who say it doesn't make any difference which way the master cylinder is connected don't know what they're talking about.

The success of your brake system comes down to compatibility and attention to detail. You must take the time to plan and buy components that are matched to the other components. Then you need to install those new and rebuilt parts in such a way that there are no leaks, no binding of the master cylinder linkage, and no chance for the lines or hoses to vibrate or chafe against a sharp edge.

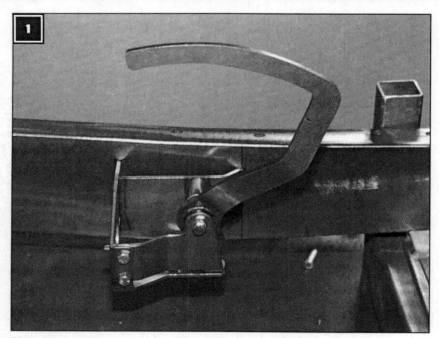

The brake pedal mount is from Deuce Factory, welded to the left frame rail and located according to the distance from the axle centerline. It's always a good idea to do a mock-up with the driver in the car before final-welding the pedal mount.

Installing the brakes on John's stretched Deuce pickup occurred over time, and parts of the installation have been covered in the suspension chapters. Yet, it seemed only fair to assemble all the brake installation information and present it here.

The Parts

Like most current street rods, this one mounts the master cylinder below the floor using a pedal mount from Deuce Factory. The master cylinder is a split reservoir unit meant for a later-model Mustang with four-wheel disc brakes. The bore measures 1 1/8 inch in diameter. Neal and John have chosen not to use a power brake booster. The bracket assembly will also mount a 1968 to 1976 Corvette master cylinder, a master meant for four-wheel disc brakes and no power booster.

The pedal pivot must be installed so it is perpendicular to the frame centerline.

The dual chamber master cylinder being used is a four-wheel-disc unit from a late-model Mustang unit.

John insisted on substantial front brakes: an 11-inch vented rotor and Wilwood Dynalite 3, four-piston calipers.

Whenever nonfloating calipers are installed, they must be centered over the rotor, usually with shims that come with the calipers.

The caliper bolts to the spindle assembly with high-quality bolts included with the calipers. If a separate bracket is used to mount the caliper, it's important to make sure the bracket leaves the caliper square to the surface of the rotor.

The front brakes use four-piston calipers, the Dynalite 3 models, carved from aluminum by Wilwood. Each caliper is mated to an 11-inch vented rotor. All the brake parts came with the suspension kit that Neal and John purchased from Heidt's.

In the rear, the Lincoln Versailles rear end came with factory disc brakes. Neal and John chose to take advantage of these OEM disc brakes and factory calipers, the ones with the integral emergency brake.

Installation

The first brake part to be attached is the master cylinder mount, which Neal tack-welds to the

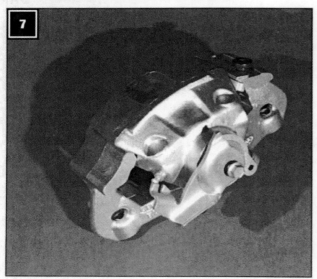

The nice thing about the Lincoln rear end Neal installed is the fact that it came with disc brakes. These single piston calipers have an integral emergency brake—note the lever on the side of the caliper.

Though hard to find, the Lincoln Versailles rear end with disc brakes makes for a neat assembly that requires no adaptations, special brackets, or second caliper for the emergency brake.

frame early in the project, well before the first mock-up is done with the pickup body. "The front to rear distance is figured from the front-axle centerline," explains Neal. "When you install these, it's important to be sure the pivot is perpendicular to the frame centerline. How high the assembly is mounted on the frame depends on the master cylinder being used. With a power booster you might have to mount it a little lower so the booster will clear the floor."

The rotors come with bearings and seals. Neal starts this part of the installation by installing the inner bearing races, packing the bearings, installing the inner wheel bearing and seal, and setting the rotor on over the spindle. The calipers mount to twin mounting points that are an integral part of the cast spindle assembly. Though the spindle mounts and the Wilwood calipers are designed to work together, the installer still needs to ensure that the caliper is centered over the rotor. The calipers come with a series of small spacers that are used to shim the caliper and center it over the rotor.

The calipers mount to the spindles with two bolts supplied with the kit. Because so much force

is transmitted through these mounting bolts to the chassis, it's important to use either the supplied bolts or replacements of equal or greater strength.

In the rear Neal simply replaced the "used" calipers with rebuilt components. "These calipers are kind of expensive," explains Neal. "If you didn't have the old cores it might pay to buy some rusty calipers at the swap meet and use those as cores, because otherwise the auto parts store will charge you a hefty core charge."

The plumbing of the brakes is covered in more detail in Chapter 7. The truck will be plumbed with stainless lines throughout, with braided No. 3 flexible lines at each wheel.

*C*hoosing brakes is one of the most important and most difficult parts of the building process. There are no easy answers to commonly asked questions. For help with the questions and quandaries of choosing brakes we asked Shane, SO-CAL foreman, for some insight into the way they pick components for the cars they build.

"Typically in our end of the deal, 50 percent of the choice is based on appearance. The highboy roadster guys like the SO-CAL front brake kit (note: there's a new matching rear brake kit available as well), so that dictates what goes on the front. Other guys will opt for something like a Magnum disc brake kit. But then there's that true die-hard guy who needs early-Ford brakes or early-Ford brakes with Buick drums.

"When we plan a car the first consideration is, how hard does the customer drive? We have to design the brakes around the car and the way it's driven.

"Weight is a factor too. A lightweight car like our roadster doesn't need as much brakes as a '55 Chevy. None of our SO-CAL roadsters have power brakes. We use a manual, 15/16-diameter, Ford Mustang master cylinder, made for disc and drum brakes. That master cylinder with the Pete and Jake's pedal ratio, and our front and rear brakes, works just great.

"Ninety-nine percent of the cars that we build use drum brakes on the rear. For the street rod market, you don't need discs in the rear. If you were driving these cars hard or on a race track that would be different. But on the street you end up turning the pressure to the rear brakes down anyway. So why do you want more brakes on the rear?

"There are exceptions of course. On my Willys I have the engine set way back, and huge tires on the rear with skinny tires on the front. In that scenario you want the rears to work as well as the fronts. And the extended cab pickup we just finished, that has a Kugel independent rear end that came with disc brakes, so that has discs on the rear as well.

"For someone building their own car, I would suggest they consider the aesthetics first, especially on the front of an open-wheeled car. Do they want early- or late-style brakes, low- or high-tech? Now, how does that relate to the rear? Do they want to run disc or drum in the rear?

"The second thing to consider is the application. Is the choice feasible? Is the owner going vintage roadracing? Will the brakes be adequate for the intended use?

"Third, pick a reliable vendor and buy the brakes from that one vendor. Your life depends on those brakes. Don't buy calipers from one guy and rotors from another and then make up your own caliper brackets. The Bell helmet people used to have an ad that said, 'Buy a $10 helmet if you've got a $10 head.' It's like that. This is really important. Rely on the vendor for things like the master cylinder diameter and whether or not you need a power booster. If you buy a brake kit from us, for example, we recommend a particular master cylinder because we know it works with our calipers and drums."

Chapter 7

Hardware

The subject of nuts and bolts, something that seems at first so very simple, could easily be the topic of two or three separate books. In fact the fastener specifications used by NASA and the military do indeed fill volumes.

The trick of course is to remember that we're not building space shuttles, only hot rods. This doesn't mean that we don't need good bolts, lines, and hardware, because we do. Where the space shuttle might be assembled with titanium fasteners, grade-8 steel is good enough for nearly anything we can bolt together on our hot rods.

So What's a Bolt?

Simply put, a bolt is nothing more than a threaded fastener designed to screw into a hole or nut with matching female threads. But let's get a little nomenclature out of the way first. Technically a bolt is a fastener without a washer face under the head, while a cap screw has a washer face under the head. For the purposes of this chapter, male threaded fasteners will be called bolts.

More bolt terms and definitions:
• Minor diameter: the diameter measured at the smallest point, the bottom of the threads on either side

A quality cap screw has a raised surface under the head that bears on the surface it is tightened against. A good bolt or cap screw also has the head affixed at exactly 90 degrees to the centerline of the shank.

108

- Major diameter: the diameter measured at the largest point, the tops of the threads on either side
- Shank: the unthreaded part of the bolt's shaft
- Bearing surface: the raised and polished portion just under the head of a quality bolt or cap screw
- Length: measurement from the lower edge of the bearing surface, or the bottom of the head, to the end of the bolt
- Grip length: the length of the unthreaded portion
- Thread length: the length of the threaded portion of the bolt

Load, Stress, and Strain

Before looking too closely at exactly how good a grade-8 bolt is, we need to look at the types of loads that bolts are subjected to and how those loads are measured.

Technically the *load*, measured in pounds, is the force that is placed on a bolt or the force the bolt is subjected to as it resists an external force (and you thought it was your brother-in-law!).

Bolt descriptions are often followed by a psi figure. A good steel bolt might be rated at 150,000 psi. The pounds per square inch figure is derived by dividing the load in pounds by the cross-sectional area of the bolt. This is known as the *stress* within the bolt.

If you put enough load on a bolt it will change dimension, if only very slightly, and that change in dimension is known as the *strain*.

As you continue to increase the stress on a bolt it will continue to change dimension, but not in a nice linear manner. At lower levels of stress the bolt will "snap" back to its original dimension when the stress is removed. Beyond a certain point, however, the metal will have been stretched so far that it is unable to snap back. It's that point we've all experienced, that point where you feel the bolt "give."

The give that's communicated through the wrench to your hand is known as the *yield point*. The bolt has stretched so far that it can't snap back to its original dimension. In most cases if a bolt reaches its yield point and you don't tighten it further, the bolt can be screwed out of the hole or out of the nut, and the bolt may look just fine. But a very close inspection will reveal that the bolt is now longer than it was originally. Even if you can't detect the change with the naked eye, the bolt should be tossed in the trash.

If you continue to increase the stress past the yield point, the bolt will continue to stretch until it can stretch no farther. The *ultimate tensile strength* is the point at which the bolt breaks.

All of this makes a bit more sense when you consider it graphically. At lower stress levels, the

Nuts with the integral synthetic collar make good lock nuts and are available in stainless or chrome plated. The only downside is the fact that the collar eventually "wears out."

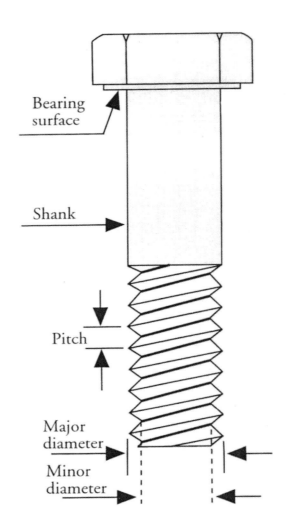

Though we think of them all as bolts, a "cap screw" is a higher-quality fastener that includes a *bearing surface* under the head.

109

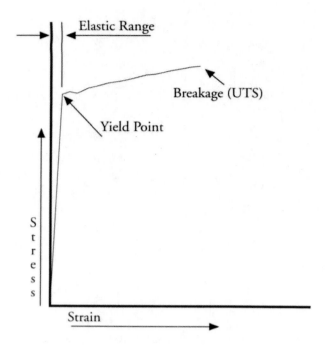

Elastic Range

Breakage (UTS)

Yield Point

Stress

Strain

With a graph it's perhaps easier to understand how increases in strain, up to the yield point, have no impact on the bolt's original dimension, even after the strain is removed. Increases beyond the yield point, however, will result in a bolt that's deformed or ruptured.

graph of bolt stress versus strain is a nice straight line. Increases in stress create proportional increases in strain. Everything is nice and predictable until the line going uphill across the graph takes a sharp turn to the right.

The point at which the stress and strain graph goes to hell is the yield point. It is the point at which the bolt will not come back to its original dimension when the stress is removed. The metal has deformed at the molecular level and will continue to deform further with greater and greater amounts of stress, until the point of rupture.

Though most of us don't think about it (at least I never did) we want to tighten the bolt, or bolt and nut combination, until we've created a strain on the bolt, but not so far that we've exceeded the yield point (more on this later). Once past the yield point we've gone past what is often called the elastic limit, meaning again that the bolt will never snap back *to its original size.*

Types of Stress

Bolts, or bolts and nuts, are asked to handle two very different types of loads. In the case of a cylinder head bolt, tightening the bolt to 100 foot-pounds puts enormous *tension* on the bolt. There is no side-to-side movement of the head. The bolt's job is to clamp the head in place and hold it

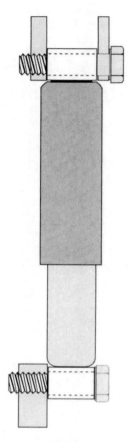

Though single shear applications, like the bottom of this shock mounting, are common on street cars, the double-shear mounting at the top is much stronger.

there against the enormous pressure of compression and combustion.

If the bolt in question is holding an upper suspension arm in place, or locates the shock absorber in place, then there is very little tension on the bolt; the load in this case is trying to *shear* the bolt into pieces.

Most of the bolts we use on our hot rods are loaded in tension. We are clamping something together with little or no side load. It's interesting to note that most bolts are only about 60 percent as strong in shear as they are in tension. We should also consider that shear can be further subdivided into single and double. A double-shear joint is much, *much stronger* than a single-shear joint (see the illustration for clarification).

Bolts That Get Tired

The subject of stress leads to the related concept of fatigue, the idea that even if the bolt doesn't break when you torque it down, it might break six months later after a couple of million "on and off" cycles. To illustrate, a coat hanger doesn't break the first time you bend it. No, it breaks after 10 or 20 cycles of bending back and forth.

High-quality bolts are designed to resist fatigue through the use of good alloys, high-quality manufacture and heat treatment, and good design. A good bolt has carefully manufactured threads and the correct heat treatment at the right point in the bolt's genesis. It's important that the head be exactly perpendicular to the bolt's axis (even an error of just a few degrees increases stress within the bolt enormously) and that the threads blend smoothly into the unthreaded shank of the bolt.

How Bolts Are Made

Most quality bolts are made in a rolling or forming operation. The raw stock or "wire" is rolled through special dies that form the threads without any cutting. Though the method may seem odd, the reasons bolts are made this way are numerous and hard to refute.

First, cutting threads is very time-consuming. Second, cutting leaves rough edges behind, while a quality rolling operation actually leaves a smooth, polished surface. Third, cutting threads means cutting across the grain of the bolt, making it much weaker. Rolling threads, on the other hand, encourages the grain to flow with the threads. Also, the rolling operation compresses or forges the surface of the threads, making them much stronger.

Less expensive bolts are made from mild steel, steel with a low percentage of carbon (ignoring stainless and exotic bolts for now). Bolts of this nature are weak and also very malleable. By adding a higher percentage of carbon the strength of the material goes up, but so does the brittleness. This is a costly trade-off when it comes to bolts loaded in tension, which need to retain some of their springiness to be effective.

Good bolts are commonly made from medium carbon steel with other additives that provide strength without making the material too brittle or glasslike. One such additive is manganese; another popular combination is chromium and molybdenum (chrome-moly). Good raw material in combination with careful heat treating can create bolts that are both strong and forgiving.

It's important not only that the bolt be heat treated, but that it be heat treated before the thread rolling is done. Heat treating done after the threads are formed tends to anneal or normalize the compressed surface of the threads created by the dies, essentially undoing the "forging" that was done during the thread forming process.

Thread Specifications

What we often call NC and NF (national course and national fine) are actually UNC and UNF (unified national course and unified national fine). This system came out of the confusion that arose during World War II when English mechanics tried to repair American airplanes with Whitworth (a British thread standard) nuts and bolts. The ensuing troubles convinced the allies that they needed some type of unified thread form. The "unified" system they settled on retained most of the existing American standards and specifications.

For those of us who still work within this American or unified system (as opposed to the metric system), those standards developed 50 years ago

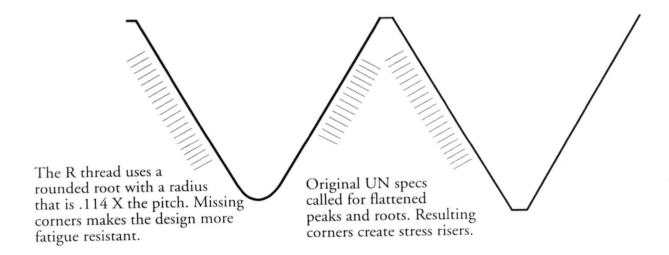

The R thread uses a rounded root with a radius that is .114 X the pitch. Missing corners makes the design more fatigue resistant.

Original UN specs called for flattened peaks and roots. Resulting corners create stress risers.

The specifications for an R thread call for a rounded root of specific radius. The idea is to eliminate the corners and thus the stress risers.

Just add two to the number of marks on the head to get the grade of a bolt or cap screw. Symbols and letters usually indicate the manufacturer. Grade 2 and 3 usually aren't marked.

are still valid. There has been some evolution of the thread specifications since those first specifications were written, but most of those have to do with the radius at the base of the thread. For example, a sharp V-shaped notch at the base of the threads makes an ideal stress riser—a spot where the bolt is likely to fatigue and break. Most of the better bolts now specify an "R" thread which simply spells out a specific radius at the bottom of the thread (see the illustration for a better explanation of the R thread).

How Strong Is Strong?

As we explained, bolts are measured in pounds per square inch of tension or stress. The ultimate tensile strength, or UTS, is the point at which the bolt breaks. The other specification given for quality bolts is the yield point, the point at which the bolt will no longer bounce back to its original dimension once the stress is removed.

A grade-2 bolt, sometimes called a hardware-store bolt, is rated at 74,000-psi UTS up to a size of 3/4 inch. This same bolt has a yield strength of 57,000 psi.

Moving up the scale, a grade-5 bolt, the point where good bolts start, is rated at 120,000-psi UTS and has a published yield point of 92,000 psi. Grade-5 bolts are considered good enough for most general purpose automotive use, engine covers, and light double-shear duty. These bolts can

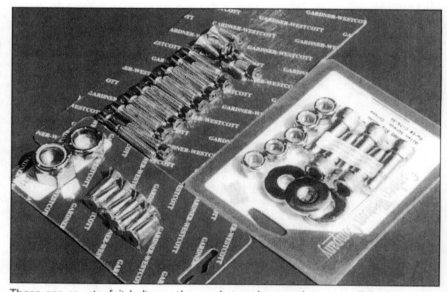

There are counterfeit bolts on the market and some that are polished and thus have no markings. It pays to buy Made-in-USA bolts from a supplier you trust, or to rely on known brands like Gardner Westcott and ARP.

be identified by the three radial dashes found on the head.

What many of us consider the ultimate bolt, the grade-8 bolt, is rated at 150,000-psi and 130,000-psi yield strength. These can be used in heavy-duty double-shear applications, assuming the shank is the correct size for the hole it's being inserted into. A grade-8 bolt is generally considered an upgrade for engine assembly situations. Some builders get to a certain point where they simply don't want to use anything of lesser quality. Grade-8 bolts have six radial dashes on their head.

Chrome "Allen" bolts come in a variety of head styles, including the popular button head. Buttons must be used with discretion as the shallow socket head won't allow them to be tightened as much.

There are a variety of fasteners with UTS ratings of well over 200,000 psi. Aircraft and aerospace often require bolts with these higher ratings. In automotive use the most common application for these very high-strength fasteners is connecting rod bolts, which may have a rating of 260,000 psi or more, especially for competition applications.

Allen Bolts

Universally known as "Allen" bolts (Allen is actually a trade name), socket-headed cap screws (SHCS) are loved by many hot rodders and most motorcycle nuts. The small head can be an advantage in many situations, but most of us use them for their apparent precision and the feel of "machinery" they lend to anything they touch.

Though many books state that all SHCS bolts are at least 170,000 psi for UTS, or better than a grade-8 bolt, this fact is no longer true. Like all the other hardware you buy, you now have to be careful where, and from whom, you buy your SHCS bolts. In particular, the chrome-plated variety are often only about a grade-5, but you don't know unless you ask. You also have to realize that these bolts often come with relatively long threads, which may have to be shortened with a die-grinder or hacksaw.

The other little problem with these bolts is the small size of the head, meaning it's hard to use the full strength of the bolt to clamp things together. And if you use a standard washer under the head it will deform later, leaving you with a loose bolt. The answer is to use a hardened and ground washer under the head of the "Allen" bolt.

The only thing sexier than an SHCS is one with a button head. These little rounded heads look like rivets. The problem is the fact that the button head allows for only a very shallow socket that won't let you get a good grip with the wrench. So don't use the button heads if you need serious clamping pressure.

The only people who like these socket-headed cap screws more than hot rodders are custom Harley-Davidson builders; it follows then that any good Harley-Davidson dealership or aftermarket shop will have a great selection of these bolts.

Chrome plating a bolt weakens it slightly. Compensation is provided by the fact that these are generally very strong bolts to start with. Anyone who has used these bolts soon discovers that rust often develops down inside the head, because the chrome-plating process just can't get plating down into those crevices. To make it worse, if the heads point up they hold water! The answer is to use the little chrome caps that snap into the socket, or to put a dab of clear silicon on the end of the wrench the first time the bolt is used.

You can have your own bolts chrome plated, but considering the availability of already-chromed bolts, it's not a good trade-off. While the nickel and chrome plating aren't very thick, the process does add to the dimensions of the threads, and that shiny bolt you just had plated might stick when it goes into the hole (or more likely, when you try to screw it out). If you do have a bolt chrome plated, be sure to mask off the threads so they don't grow in size.

113

If in doubt about any bolt or nut, it's a good idea to chase the threads with a tap or die. If the die is doing much cutting, then there's a problem with the bolt and the best approach is to look for a replacement.

Stainless Bolts

A discussion of stainless bolts is one of those topics sure to start an argument at the rod run or in the local tavern. Many builders swear by stainless fasteners. They love the look and the fact that they never rust. You might say that chrome bolts never rust, but there's always the issue of flaking chrome, or the way the inside of the Allen heads always seems to rust. There's no problem with rust in the head of a stainless Allen, because there is no coating. If you suggest that the stainless bolts aren't as strong, their proponents respond, "I use grade-8 stainless and they're great!"

If you add chromium to steel you get the material we commonly refer to as stainless steel. The 300 series stainless steels are some of the most common; a typical example might contain 18 percent chromium and 9 percent nickel, in addition to a small percentage of carbon. While 300 series stainless bolts are resistant to corrosion (they are often called CRES in the industry, or Corrosion Resistant), they are not as strong as a grade-5 bolt. Most fastener-industry charts place them somewhere between a grade 2 and a grade 5, with a UTS of roughly 85,000 psi and a yield strength of only about 35,000 psi.

There are stainless bolts rated to more than 200,000-psi UTS, but most of these are 400 series and are not commonly encountered in shops where we buy our bolts. The other problem with these 400 series stainless bolts is the fact that they rust!

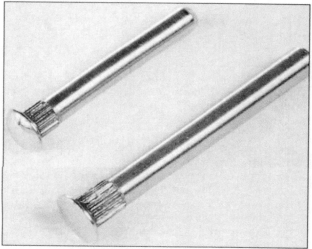

A good use of stainless steel—door hinge pins for 1932 Fords and other vehicles. *Deuce Factory*

Stainless bolts also work-harden in service. What all this means is that stainless bolts are best used for light-load situations. The fact that they stretch easily and work-harden in service means that some builders insist on using them only once (more controversy). Stainless threads also tend to gall, so it's a good idea to use Loctite or anti-seize compound to minimize metal to metal contact at the surface of the threads.

What Keeps It Tight

You might think that the lock washer is what keeps the nut on the bolt, or the bolt in the hole. Actually what keeps the bolt from unscrewing itself is friction between the male and female threads. By tightening the bolt to somewhere near the yield point, we have in effect stretched the threads. This stretch keeps the tension on the bolt and the friction intact between the male and female threads. Most locking washers and nuts work not so much by "locking" the nut but rather by maintaining this tension between the threads.

Because stronger bolts have a higher yield point, we can tighten the grade-8 bolt *tighter* than the grade-5 bolt (assuming the female half of this relationship is up to the task) and create more friction and more tension in the bolt.

The tension that keeps the bolt tight can also be the bolt's undoing. Consider the threads as a ramp wound around an axis. When you tighten the bolt you are using mechanical force to move a load "uphill." No matter how tight the bolt is, there will always be a tendency for anything on that ramp to slide downhill.

It takes only a few degrees of rotation to eliminate the stress within a tightened bolt. What this means is that the cotter key that "keeps" the nut on the ball joint, or the safety wire used in competition, is meant primarily to keep the bolt and nut from falling off altogether once they become loose. The cotter key won't keep the bolt tight.

What will help to keep the bolt tight is a Nyloc-type lock nut, an all-metal lock nut, a good split ring lock washer, one nut "jammed" up against the other, or a drop of Loctite properly applied. Loctite comes in a confusing array of grades, some meant for light-duty work, others meant for parts that will never be unscrewed again.

Most of us think of Loctite as "blue or red." Red is meant for heavy-duty applications while blue is for smaller and presumably less-important applications. The blue Loctite most commonly encountered in an automotive shop is either number 242 or 243. Both are considered "a medium strength threadlocker for fasteners up to 3/4 inch." Number 243 has a slight advantage in that it's slightly stronger than 242, is quicker to set, and is more tolerant of a little oil on the threads. The common red 262 Loctite is a "high-strength threadlocker" and will require "extra effort and possibly heat for removal."

No matter which one you use they work best on clean threads, and require free metal ions and an oxygen-free atmosphere to work. What this means is that oily threads should be cleaned with Loctite's own Clean 'n Prime, or something that leaves no residue behind, like Brake Klean.

Nuts and Other Female Threads

A bolt or cap screw isn't worth a damn without a matching set of female threads. Those threads might come in the form of threads cut in a casting, or a nut with female threads designed to match those on the bolt.

Most of us have been taught that "a fine-thread bolt is stronger than a coarse-threaded bolt of the same size and rating." That statement is true when you have a bolt and nut combination clamping something together. The fine-thread bolt and nut are stronger because the minor diameter of the bolt is larger than it would be for a coarse-threaded bolt, and because there is more net contact between the threads on the bolt and the nut.

The fly in the ointment comes when a high-quality 170,000-psi bolt is screwed into a casting made from iron or aluminum. Now we have a mismatch between the strength of the material the bolt is made from and the material the casting is made

from. In order to compensate for the fact that the steel is much stronger than the cast iron or aluminum, the threads in the casting are often cut in a coarse thread. The larger, coarse threads in the casting increase the shear strength of those threads, making for a stronger assembly. Coarse threads are also better suited to the coarser texture of many of these cast materials.

Final Words of Wisdom

After 30-some years of turning wrenches, both as a professional and an amateur, it's embarrassing to realize that I've been doing many of the wrong things to bolts for much of that time. What follows are a few of those mistakes.

Don't cut "just one more thread" on that bolt. We've explained the care that goes into the manufacture of a good bolt—don't undo all that craft by cutting more threads. If it's the only bolt you have for the job and it's too long, then put a washer or two under the head until you can get out and buy the correct bolt.

Don't torque a stud down into the casting. The threads at the bottom of the tapped hole are rounded slightly due to the shape of the tap (even if they are cut with a bottoming tap). When you torque the stud into the hole, you put all the force on those few bottom threads. Studs should be screwed in finger tight. Use Loctite if necessary to keep the stud in

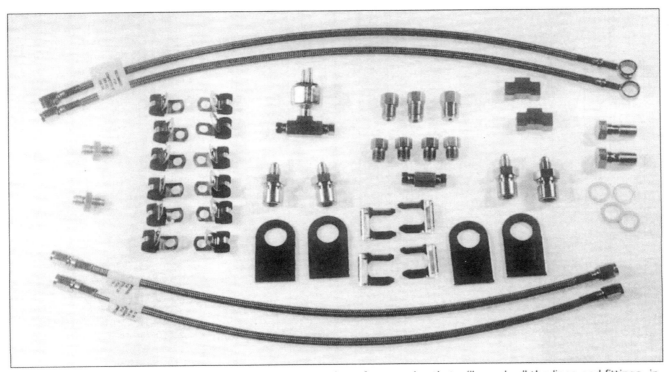

When it comes time to plumb the chassis, there are a number of companies that will supply all the lines and fittings, in either 45-degree or 37-degree AN, precut and bent to fit your particular situation. *Pure Choice Motorsports*

Stainless steel through-frame fittings like these make the job of plumbing the frame with brake lines much neater. *Deuce Factory*

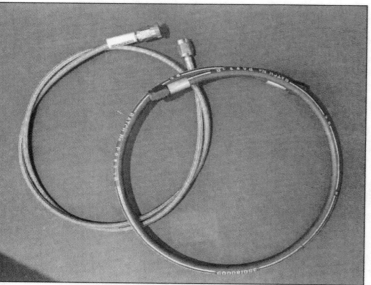

Braided high-pressure hoses with Teflon inner liners, often used as brake lines, come in common sizes like –02, –03, and –04. Remember that the braid will act like a saw on anything it touches, which is why some hoses are available with plastic sheathing covering the braid.

place. Some mechanics go so far as to drop a small ball bearing down into the hole and then screw the stud down finger tight until it contacts the bearing.

Don't use bolts with long, threaded shanks in shear applications. Buy one of the better cap screws, maybe even an AN, MS (military specifications), or NAS bolt from the airport, with the

proper nonthreaded shank of the right length and the right diameter.

A bolt should be long enough, whether used in shear or tension, that when the nut is fully tightened, there is at least one full thread protruding from the end of the nut.

Anytime you're in doubt, take the time to use a torque wrench. When you're torquing a bolt, consider that much of the torque used to tighten a bolt is actually used to overcome friction between the male and female threads, and not to put the correct amount of stress on the bolt. Any dirt on the threads increases the friction, so be sure the threads are clean.

The other point worth repeating is to always use anti-seize on the threads of chrome and stainless bolts.

Plumbing
The Basics

When it comes to moving the common liquids around under the hood, the aftermarket now provides a vast number of choices. Yes, you can still use the good old OEM stuff or the materials available at the local Pep Boys store. There's nothing wrong with that as long as you use quality materials and install them with care.

When it comes to plumbing, however, more and more builders of hot rods are looking for an upgrade. Driven by a desire for quality and certain aesthetic considerations, many builders want braided hose with anodized aluminum ends. Companies like Earl's, Aeroquip, and others provide high-quality hoses with or without the braided stainless covers, with matching ends. Both the hose and the hose ends are available as extremely high-quality components suitable for competition, or in three or four less stringent grades more suitable for street use.

First we have to back up and explain that much of this high-end hose market started as surplus from the military, and thus uses what is commonly called the AN (Air Corps/Navy) measuring system. AN fittings all have 37-degree flares instead of the more common 45-degree flares used in most American OEM lines and fittings. Hose sizes are often indicated by one or two digits, all of which makes sense when you realize there is a method to the madness.

Common AN line sizes are "dash three," "dash four," and so forth. *Dash three* is generally written "–03". So what does that mean in the real world? The 3 is the numerator of a fraction with 16 as the denominator. So, –03 equals 3/16 inch. It gets a little confusing because the 3/16 doesn't indicate the exact inside diameter (I.D.) or even the outside diameter (O.D.) of the line. When the system was first implemented, each size was designed to replace an existing hard-metal line with a flexible

Designed to work with the reusable hose ends, this AQP Racing hose can be used with fuel, oil, or coolant, in temperatures from 55 degrees below zero to 300 degrees Fahrenheit. Available sizes run from –04 to –32. *Aeroquip*

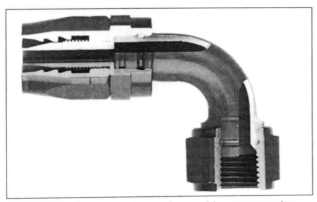

This cutout shows one type of reusable compression-style hose end. Specific hose ends need to be used with specific hoses, all designed as part of the same system. *Aeroquip*

line of about the same I.D. Thus, –03 has about the same I.D. as a standard 3/16-inch brake line. Get it? A dash four (–04) has the same internal diameter as a 4/16-, or 1/4-inch steel line.

Getting the Hose

The hose you use depends primarily on the fluid being moved, the pressure of the liquid, and exactly how trick you want the finished product to be.

In the case of water hoses, there's nothing wrong with using molded hoses from the local auto parts store. If you know the size of the inlet and outlet and the approximate shape (you can even bend up a template with a piece of wire or coat hanger), most counter workers will help you find the right molded hose from among their substantial stock. The key is to use brand-name hoses and avoid the tendency to force the hose into something other than the pre-formed shape, as most hoses will collapse at that point.

The stainless outer braid most of us are so enamored of is available raw, as are the colored hose "ends" (which are actually covers for the stainless hose clamps) that go along with the braided stainless look. This way you can buy molded hoses and then cover them with braided stainless. The braid does more than provide that nice race-car look. The stainless covering also protects the hose from abrasion.

What you want to avoid are the corrugated radiator hoses, for aesthetic reasons if no other. If you have to run the water a long distance, straight pipe can be used with rubber "connectors" at either

AN-style fittings for fuel, oil, and coolant lines come in various shapes and configurations, some *designed for a crimped* collar, some for a hose clamp, and some for a do-it-yourself compression-type connection. *Aeroquip*

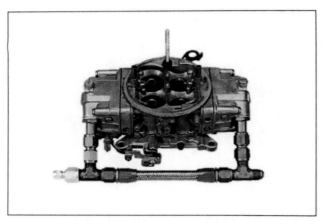

These very neat, high-quality fuel manifolds are available pre-assembled for most popular carburetors. *Aeroquip*

end. It's important that any hard line like this have beaded ends so the clamped ends can't slip off. Any good radiator shop can make up a straight section of tubing and also do a nice job of beading the ends.

Like water hoses, flexible gas lines can be made up of the black neoprene hose available at the local auto parts store. Because current fuels have so many new additives, it's important to use only current, brand-name fuel lines. In most cases fuel line like this will slip over a simple barbed fitting where it's secured with a hose clamp. Remember, EFI systems run far more fuel pressure in the lines than was experienced in any part of a carbureted fuel system, so pick your fuel lines and clamps accordingly. Upgrades in fuel lines include a variety of reinforced and braided hoses available from the aftermarket, most of which use brand-specific anodized ends.

These ends could be a book chapter in themselves. A little time spent with an Aeroquip or Earl's catalog will open your eyes to the huge selection of hoses and ends available. As stated earlier, the very best are good enough for competition use. At the other end of this aftermarket hose-end selection are the simple barbed fittings. But unlike the stuff from the auto parts store, these fittings are anodized in red or blue and look great when used with a stainless over-braid and clamp cover of the same color.

Remember that for many carburetor applications, fuel manifolds are available pre-assembled from a variety of sources. Fuel lines for Holley carburetors or a standard three-deuces setup are only a phone call away.

As always, you need to make sure the hose you use is intended to handle the application, be it gas, oil, or the high-pressure line to the power steering gear. The lines used between the auto-

matic transmission and the cooler, for example, are designed specifically for transmission fluid. If you use something besides a barbed hose end, be sure it is matched to the hose brand and size. High-quality hose ends come in various configurations so be sure the one you buy is the one you want, and follow the manufacturer's directions for assembly and testing of the hose.

Brake Hoses

If you assemble a radiator hose from aftermarket parts and it blows later while cruising down the highway, you've created a mess and an inconvenience. In the worst case, you could damage the engine if the temperature is allowed to go too high before you shut it down. If the same thing happens with a brake hose, you've created more than an inconvenience.

The only truly approved hard line for brakes is the OEM-style steel hose with double-flared 45-degree fittings. Hot rodders often lean toward the stainless steel hose with 37-degree single-flare AN fittings. Though aesthetics drive much of these decisions, there's also the "I want this car to have the best of everything" mentality at work here, along with the related refrain, "I want this car to last forever."

Yes, a stainless line will last "forever," but in reality a standard steel line will last nearly that long. Working from personal experience, it's obvious that steel lines commonly last a minimum of 15 to 20 years even when the car is used daily in Minnesota's salt-infested winter driving environment.

When it comes to the flexible brake hoses, a similar dilemma arises. The DOT-approved hoses are the big, ugly black ones. The hoses everyone wants to use are the braided stainless hoses with anodized or polished ends. These braided hoses are made up of a Teflon liner inside a stainless braided cover. The hose can be purchased raw from companies like Earl's and Aeroquip, or pre-assembled hoses can be purchased with a variety of ends factory installed. Most of these are rated at a minimum of 2,000-psi operating pressure and a burst pressure of more than 10,000 psi.

For most brake applications, a –03 hose is the right size. Clutch hydraulic systems probably require a –04 because they are moving a larger volume of brake fluid. Call me conservative, but I recommend buying the hoses factory assembled with the ends already installed. They can be ordered in nearly any length; if you can't get exactly the right fitting on the end, a whole raft of adapters is available to convert the pipe fitting thread in the caliper to the AN fitting on the brake line (for example).

A few final notes on brake lines and fittings. Pay attention to the flare—don't try to mate a

37-degree hose with a 45-degree fitting on the caliper or chassis. Yes, the materials are soft and will probably "give" enough to mate the two, but seepage and failure are likely results. If you have to mate the typical American 45-degree system with the AN 37-degree system, conversion fittings are available to do just that.

Be sure all the hoses you mount, especially the flexible ones, can't come in contact with a suspension member or the edge of the tire as the suspension goes from full extension to full compression, or as the tires go from lock to lock. If you run the lines inside the frame, don't put any connectors where you can't see them and be sure to test for leaks. Leak testing is part of the installation process. When everything is finished and the system is bled, get someone to literally stand on the brake pedal while you carefully crawl around underneath with a light inspecting every fitting for any sign of leakage.

Whether you run the lines inside the frame or outside, they must be clamped in place. A variety of aluminum and stainless clamps are available from the aftermarket to make your installation as neat as possible.

We should mention that for individuals who don't want to spend their days measuring, cutting, and flaring stainless brake lines, companies like Pure Choice Motorsports will custom cut and flare all the lines and ship them to you ready to install.

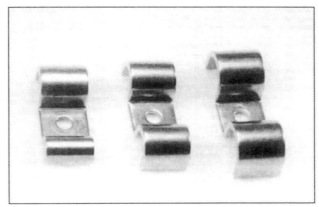

The brake lines, whether steel or stainless, must be clamped to the frame so they don't vibrate. Simple clamps like these, available in stainless, are often used to hold the lines in place. *Pure Choice Motorsports*

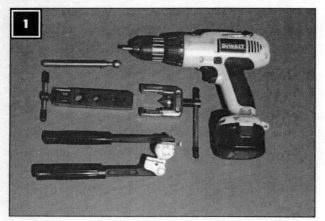

Like any other part of the building and fabrication project, plumbing the brake lines requires specialized tools. From the top: drill with deburring tool, hand deburring tool, two-part flaring tool, and high-quality tubing bender.

*A*t this point the Deuce truck frame is nearly assembled (only to be disassembled again for painting). What's left is the plumbing.

The materials Neal is using to plumb John's truck are all top-shelf. The hard lines, for example, are all 3/16 stainless. "We used lines that are 0.028-inch wall thickness," explains Neal. "These lines are seamless 304L stainless. You have to be sure the lines are seamless or they will crack when you bend or flare them. We bought ours at a local metals-supply shop, though you could also get them from a company like Pure Choice Motorsports."

The fittings are all AN 37-degree single flare, the type that use a small tube sleeve between the line nut and the flare.

Neal cuts his stainless tubing with a cut-off wheel, not a tubing cutter, because it doesn't crush the end of the tube.

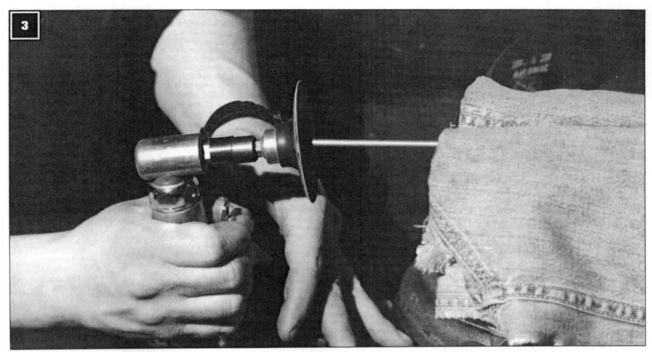

A small sander is used to clean up the end and ensure it is cut 90 degrees to the centerline of the tubing.

Neal deburrs the inside of the cut-off end. It's also a good idea to clean up the outside diameter of the tubing at the cut with a small file or some sandpaper (not shown).

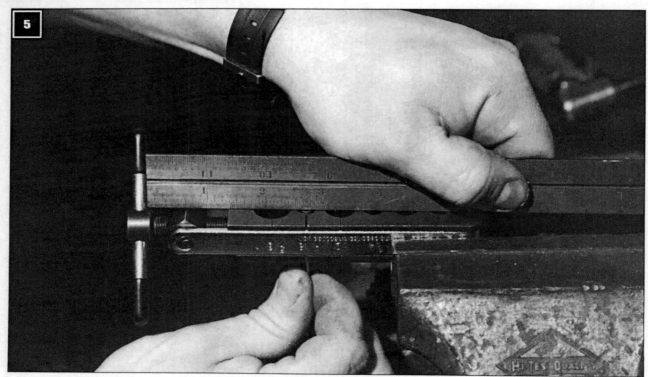

Neal uses a straightedge to make sure the tubing comes up through the clamp part of the flaring tool. The end of the tube should be flush with the top surface.

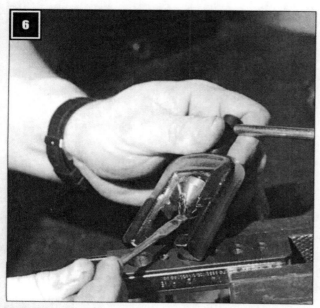

A little lube placed on the cone of the flaring tool means it's less likely to gall against the stainless. Stainless doesn't flare and bend easily, and thus requires quality tools and attention to detail if it's to be used effectively.

The four flex hoses are —03 braided with the Teflon inner liner. Neal bought these from a local supply company with the ends installed, though they're also available from high-performance retailers. A few adapters were required, like the 1/8-inch pipe to No. 3 AN for the front Wilwood calipers, and the 7/16-inch banjo to No. 3 AN for the Lincoln calipers used on the rear of the truck.

The installation is made easier by Neal's careful attention to detail and by his use of high-quality tools. "Imperial Eastman or Parker make some pretty good bending tools," says Neal. "They help you to do a nice, neat job. A good single-tubing bender will probably cost you $45 or $50, but you get smaller bend radii out of that tool. My bender will bend a 3/16-inch tube to a 5/8-inch radius. That's a good size for a project like this, and about as tight as you can go without collapsing the tube."

Fabrication of each section of tubing starts by cutting the tubing to length. If you're new to this notion of cutting, bending, and installing brake lines you might want to mock up the whole thing in standard 3/16-inch steel line, or even some heavy welding rod material. That way you can

As Neal explains, "The flaring tool is tightened down against the end of the tubing until you feel the metal stop moving."

figure out the exact length you need, taking into account the amount needed for each bend.

Neal does the actual cutting with an air-powered cut-off wheel, being careful to make the cut square. After cutting the tube, he carefully dresses and deburrs both the outside and the inside of the tube. Neal goes on to explain, "You can use a standard tubing cutter but it tends to squash the tubing and the size of the hole ends up pretty small." After cutting the tubing to size, the outside of each cut is cleaned up with a small file while the inside is deburred with the appropriate tool.

Now it's time to flare the tubing, which must be done with a quality flaring tool designed for a 37-degree single flare, not the 45-degree double flare seen on most American OEM applications.

Neal warns that "the end of the tube needs to be really clean without any nicks or burrs. You can use a lubricant of some kind between the cone and the tube so it won't gall against the tubing. The cone of the

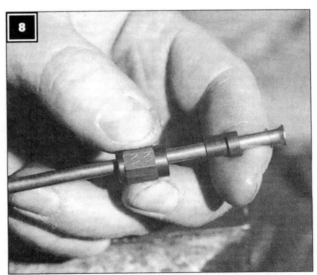

Here's the properly flared stainless tube with the sleeve and the AN nut behind it.

123

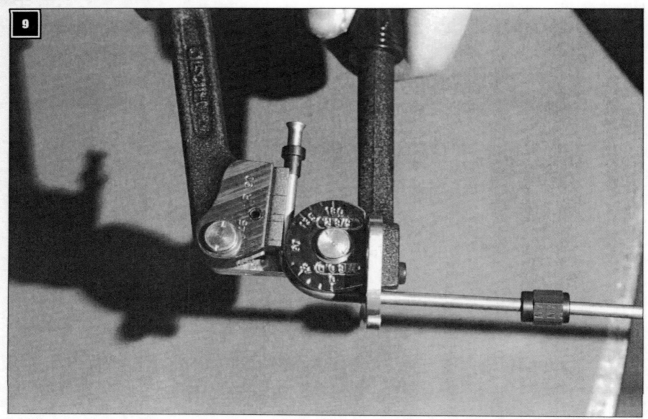

In order to make a nice 90-degree bend, Neal actually takes the tubing past 90 degrees because there is always some "spring back" when he take the pressure off the tool.

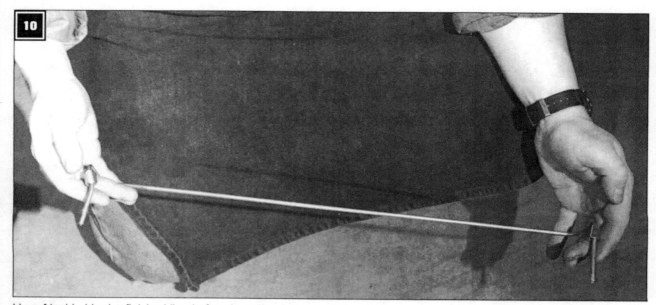

Here Neal holds the finished line before installing it on the frame.

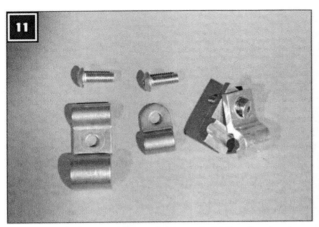

A variety of clamps are available to hold the line in place along the frame.

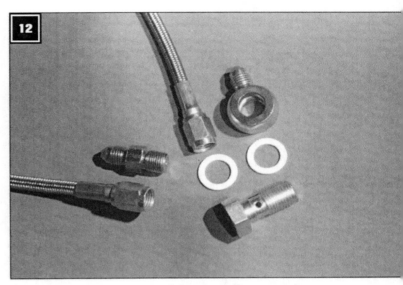

Fittings and adapters are available that will convert the pipe and banjo fittings found on many calipers to the 37-degree AN system.

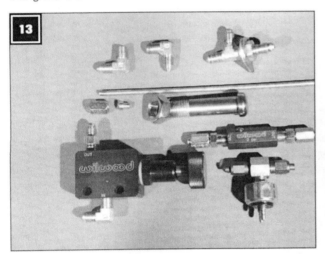

The complete installation requires a 2-pound residual pressure valve in the line to both the front and the rear brakes as well as a proportioning valve in the line to the rear brakes. Also shown are a few of the fittings used to complete the job.

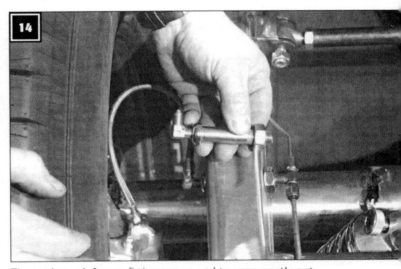

These through-frame fittings are used to very neatly get the line on the other side of the frame, where it generally attaches to a flexible hose or line.

flaring tool needs to be nice and clean, without any nicks. On better tools the cones can be replaced, and if you use the tool a lot you might need to do that."

The tubing is positioned in the clamp part of the flaring tool so the end is flush with the top surface of the tool. Neal says you have to exert pressure, by turning the cone down against the tubing, until "you can't go any further." Remember that the tubing will be damaged if you continue to exert pressure after it has been fully flared out against the clamp. This is the time to install the nut and the tubing sleeve, from the other end, before doing the second flare.

The nuts that are part of this AN system are made from steel, with a protective coating of cadmium or zinc. Many of the fittings used here are anodized aluminum. In spite of the fact that both the steel and the aluminum are "coated," they are in fact dissimilar metals and Neal recommends the judicious use of a little anti-seize on the threads. Just remember to flush a little extra brake fluid through the lines when it comes time to bleed the brakes so any anti-seize is flushed out as well.

Instead of using one flex line at the rear end and then attaching the hard line to the axle housing, Neal attached the hard line to the frame and used a flex line at each wheel, because he *thought it was neater*

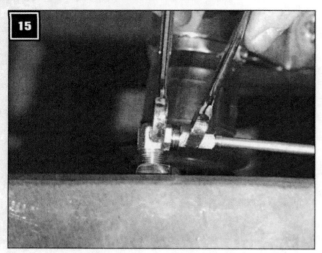

To tighten the fittings, it's important to put a wrench on both "halves" of the fitting. And you must check each one of these for possible seepage before you consider the job finished.

that way. And instead of running the hard line up and over the frame to a fitting or bracket, Neal used through-frame fittings for a very sanitary installation.

Brakes lines will vibrate and crack if not secured in place. The lines on the Deuce truck frame are held in place with small two-piece clamps. Each clamp is secured to the rail with a machine screw threaded into holes tapped in the frame rails. It's important to drill all the holes and weld on any necessary brackets now while the truck is in mock-up stage.

Plumbing the frame is pretty much a nuts and bolts kind of deal, fitting adapter A into flexible line B, the other end of which screws into another fitting and then the hard line. Like most parts of this hot-rod building project, a neat plumbing job requires patience and attention to detail. Don't skimp on materials or time. If you find the line you just bent up has the bend in the wrong place, throw it away and start over, bending and rebending may fatigue the line. At the very least, it makes for a sloppy-looking job. And that's the one thing we're trying to avoid here.

Neal likes to use the two-part line clamps seen here. Each one requires that you drill and tap a hole in the frame rail.

*I*n order to find out what professional builders are using for fasteners and plumbing in the real world, we spent a few minutes with Shane, foreman of the SO-CAL shop.

Q. Shane, are grade-5 and grade-8 good enough for most tasks encountered while building a hot rod? And where do you buy your nuts and bolts?

A. Yes, grade-5 are wonderful for almost everything. We don't like grade-8 as much because they're more brittle than the grade-5. The only time we use something like an NAS bolt (National Aerospace Standard) is when we're looking for a really trick-looking bolt or nut. We only do it for aesthetics. We buy most of our bolts from the hardware store or a fastener supplier. For the specialized stuff we use either King Bolt in Los Angeles or South Coast Specialties in Lake Havasu, Arizona.

Q: How do you feel about lock nuts?

A: We use lock nuts on anything we can. I like lock washers just as well but they tear up finishes. We try to use an AN washer and then a lock nut. The Nyloc type of lock nut is really good but guys need to be aware that after one or two uses, that nut is tired. They should do the mock-up with regular nuts so they don't wear out the Nylocs. We do like the Nylocs, but of course we can't use them on exhaust, the heat melts the nylon part of the nut. On the exhaust we use a pinch nut, a lock washer, or a jam nut. Using a second nut jammed up against the first is a real good way to go.

Q: What about plumbing under the hood, do you use a lot of the fancy braided hoses?

A: Typically we use standard rubber hoses because that's what Pete likes—standard rubber hoses for fuel with typical stainless hose clamps. For the radiator hoses we use standard Gates molded hoses. We bend up a pattern out of welding wire or lightweight "corrugated" aluminum flex-hose and take that to the parts store. They usually let us walk around behind the counter until we've found the right hose.

We use some braided lines depending on the situation. The drag racing sanctioning bodies like everything to be braided hose or hard line, so the type of hose you use depends on the intended use. Pete always says, "if you're in the middle of nowhere and need a hose it's hard to find the fancy AN stuff."

Q: What about brake lines and fittings?

A: Typically we haven't done much stainless, unless that's what the customer wants, we're always afraid the customer will have trouble finding a fitting or line if they have trouble on the road. So we use the standard mild steel brake line for most of our cars. From the frame to the rear end we use a standard rubber, OEM-style hose. Our SO-CAL brake kit includes braided hoses, but they're black-plastic covered because Pete doesn't like the look of braided.

Q: Shane, you do service on cars that other people have built, what kinds of hardware mistakes do you see on those cars?

A: Guys will have a clevis on a piece of clutch linkage, for example, and they put a bolt through it as the pivot. The problem is the bolt they use has threads along the complete length so the threads wear out the clevis and the eye and then there's too much play. It's really just because they used the wrong bolt for the pivot. They should have used a bolt with a long shoulder and then shortened the threads.

The other problem is with stainless and chrome bolts and hardware. Guys don't put anti-seize compound on chrome or stainless bolts; they have to have anti-seize on the threads. The stainless tends to gall, even when it's a stainless bolt and nut combination; stainless has a real affinity for itself.

Chrome bolts can be too big, and even if they aren't, chrome can do the same thing as stainless. Under the chrome there is nickel. If you wear through the chrome you get to the nickel, which tends to gall like the stainless does. I tell people to buy the best anti-seize they can and use lots of it.

And people don't use lock washers or lock nuts. They don't use anything and pretty soon things start to fall apart. They need to use some kind of locking device. The final thing is the guys who don't use the right length bolt so it has too much thread sticking out. It just doesn't look good, it looks sloppy.

Q: How about door latches, what does SO-CAL like to see for door latches?

A: Almost all of our cars use stock OEM factory door latches. There are a couple of exceptions, like the '51 Merc in the shop. We used late-model bear claw latches on that because the original design isn't very good. But all of our '40 Fords and Deuces use Ford latches.

The stock '32 latch works good, especially when we tweak them so they're properly adjusted and lubricated. When we first fit up the car, we take the time to make sure the door fits correctly and we stiffen up the pillars, so the door jamb doesn't just bend in when you close the door.

Chapter 8

Drivetrain

During chassis planning and construction, you have to decide not only where to put the engine, but which engine to put there. So while it might seem at first to be outside the realm of a "chassis book," we've decided to include some information designed to help you with one of the most important decisions you're going to make in planning this car. The engine choice will impact the car's character, the placement of the engine, and the type of motor mounts.

Engine Choices

The criteria for choosing an engine include cost, character, and end usage. The builder on a budget might easily settle for a late-model 350 "borrowed" from an older Caprice or discovered in the corner of a buddy's garage.

The other end of the spectrum includes a wide range of crate engines from all the major manufacturers. GM has the best-known crate-engine program, but Ford and Chrysler aren't far behind. You

For a nostalgia car, there is simply no engine with the same allure as a flathead. Like all things, the flathead has its cost, in terms of both increased maintenance and modest performance.

Seen in the SO-CAL shop, this roadster is powered by a nice new small-block—a practical motor available from your nearby Chevy dealer or an aftermarket specialist like Street and Performance.

can easily buy a new 502 from your local Chevy dealer, a high-output 460 from one of the Ford dealers, or a 528-ci Hemi from the Mopar guys.

They say that small-block Chevy engines are like bellybuttons—everyone's got one. When it comes to buying an engine, however, the small-block is easily the best value on the street. GM has produced countless millions of small-blocks, and many of those engines are still out there, just waiting to be given one more life under the hood of your personal hot rod.

The other advantage to the small-block is the relative ease of installation. Engine mounts are available in a number of different configurations, and a wide variety of transmissions, both automatic and standard, will readily bolt up. This little bow-tie engine is relatively short and has the oil pan sump at the back of the engine, both of which make it a good match for most hot rod situations.

Some cars call out for something a bit different. A nostalgia Deuce pickup like the one seen in the back of the SO-CAL shop matches up perfectly with the flathead installed between the rails. Among the many trends seen on the street of late is the tendency to look beyond the small-block for

Another Roy Brizio project, this one mates a rare Ardun overhead conversion on a flathead with a 1932 Ford.

The Ford 5.0 engine is available both new, from Ford Motorsport, and used. In either case it makes a good powerplant for a Ford hot rod.

alternative forms of power. In the GM line, these include the always-popular nail-head Buick V-8, Oldsmobile engines from the early 1950s to the end of the line, and assorted engines with the word "Cadillac" stamped on the valve cover.

Once you start to look beyond the small-block, the range of possible engines is huge. How about an old Chrysler Hemi stuffed between the rails of that new highboy, or better yet, a rare SOHC Ford V-8? Don't think you absolutely gotta install the small-block.

What's needed here is a balance between your budget, the design of the car, your mechanical skills, and your intended use of the vehicle. For the rodder who intends to drive the car extensively and requires good power and no maintenance, a GM small-block is the way to go. As mentioned before, the local dealer has a complete line of crate motors that represent great bang for the buck. For the maverick in the crowd, however, the small-block won't do. If you want to build something unusual, or want gobs of power, or love Hemis, then follow your nose down another path.

The downside to an alternative form of power is the increased cost and reduced parts availability. If you want a two-four intake for an old Hemi, be sure to bring cash. And if you want a high-lift cam for the same engine, you may have to scrounge the used parts networks, or have a stock cam reground. Engine mounts become an issue as well. Though mount kits are available for a surprising number of engines, the really old V-8s often mounted the engine at four points instead of three. Be sure you understand all the implications of using an older or unusual engine.

The other issue is one that too many people don't consider. To quote Pete Chapouris again, "People forget that these cars need maintenance just like any other vehicle." This means that hot rod motors with blowers or solid lifters require more from their owners than would a typical small-block. And

trying to find a water pump for an old Ford or Oldsmobile engine on a Sunday afternoon might mean you get to spend an extra day in Louisville.

None of which is to say the engine you install under the hood shouldn't be pure, unadulterated fun. You're not trying to build the ultimate, practical, commuter car, after all. The idea is to weigh all the ups and downs of your ideal engine choice. You need, more than anything else, a car that's usable and dependable. You also need to understand all the costs of building and operating that car.

At this point it might help to walk through a few of the crate-engine options available from Ford, GM, and Chrysler.

Ford Engines

Ford Motorsport SVO will sell you a variety of mild 302 short-blocks or complete 460 and DOHC 4.6L Cobra engines. Complete 429 Boss engines with aluminum heads are available, originally designed to run the NASCAR tracks in 1969. The most popular of the Ford offerings include the 302 long-block with high-flow GT-40 heads, and the 351 Windsor block with aluminum heads and a Victor Jr. intake manifold.

Many Ford engines have the disadvantage of a longer water pump and a front-mounted distributor/oil pump, which puts the oil pan sump at the front of the engine as well. SVO has come to your rescue with a short water pump for 289, 302, and 351W engines, and another shorty water pump designed for serpentine belt use (reverse rotation). They also sell an oil pan kit that moves the sump to the rear of the engine, eliminating interference problems with the front cross-members of many hot rods.

Mopar

The Mopar guys apparently heard that old saying that you can't beat cubic inches, because they've punched out the biggest crate Hemi to 528 cubic inches. The more sophisticated might opt instead for the V-10 Viper engine (assuming you have a larger-than-average engine compartment). Less jaded, but no less dedicated, Mopar guys will find the catalog also includes a variety of 360-ci small-blocks.

GM

GM crate motors start with a 250-horsepower 350-ci small-block available in long-block form complete with all the sheet metal. Next up is a 300-horse 350-cube crate engine. The final stop in this ladder of ascending horsepower is the ZZ4. This fourth-generation double-zee attains 355-horsepower and over 400 foot-pounds of torque. There's even a limited edition ZZ 430 rated at 430 horses from the standard 350-ci displacement.

The GM Performance Parts catalog also lists some high-tech small-blocks like the LT4, a 335

The continued popularity of the old Chrysler Hemi means new life for a design that's nearly 50 years old. Today you can buy nearly everything you need to build a 392, without going to the Sunday swap meet.

horsepower, 350-ci V-8. This engine uses a cam-driven water pump and aluminum heads with 2-inch intake valves and sodium-filled 1.55-inch exhaust valves. Combustion chambers feature fast-burn 54.4-cc combustion chambers that provide a 10.8:1 compression ratio. The relatively mild roller camshaft normally installed in this engine can be swapped for a hot LT4 camshaft good for another 20 horsepower.

Fans of the big-block haven't been forgotten. The bow-tie catalog offers 454- and 502-ci big-blocks in ratings from 425 to 502 horsepower. The 425-horse 454 uses cast-iron heads with rectangular ports and big valves mated to a cast-iron block with a roller camshaft, forged crank, and cast 8.75:1 pistons. The large displacement and modest compression mean this engine can live easily on the street burning pump-premium and still provide 500 foot-pounds of torque at 3,500 rpm.

The top of this big-block battle is the 502/502, available as a complete long-block or a complete kit. This street motor comes with big-

valve aluminum heads, roller camshaft, complete induction system, ignition system, and starter. To ensure the engine's longevity, GM engineers started with a four-bolt block, and added forged pistons, heavy-duty connecting rods, and a forged steel crankshaft.

Where to Put the Engine

Engine placement is both a topic of its own and an essential part of planning and mock-up. You need first to sketch out the logical engine location, and consider where that puts the firewall and how much room it leaves for the radiator and cooling fan(s). We all know that by setting the engine farther back, more of the weight is transferred to the rear wheels. The trade-offs include the need to install a recessed firewall, or at least notch the firewall to clear the distributor.

When Neal Letourneau did the first mock-up on the stretched Deuce pickup seen in this book, the engine proved to be a bit too far forward. During the first mock-up session, Neal and John decided to

131

If you've seen too many Ford roadsters with small-block Chevys for power, try out this 1934 Dodge with V-10 power. Built in Roy Brizio's shop, the project is the giveaway car for the Goodguys.

The small-block Chevy is a tough act to beat. They're inexpensive and readily available both new and used. Perhaps the best thing is the staggering amount of speed equipment available for the little bow-tie.

move the engine 1 inch farther back, "in order to make room for a nice big, belt-driven fan."

As you push the motor farther back, however, the bell housing and heads begin to impinge on the floor and the firewall. Once again, you're looking for balance, though when in doubt it's probably better to be too far back than not far enough.

Neal's example should be noted. If you want a car that can cruise the fairgrounds all day long without overheating, you want a big, belt-driven fan, pulling air across a nice thick radiator core, aided by a well-designed cooling shroud. What this means is that you can't have the nose of the water pump up against the inside of the radiator. Air conditioning adds another heat load to the radiator and cooling system. During the mock-up, be sure to mount a water pump and fan on the engine and be sure you make provision for the radiator shroud.

Though technically not a part of the engine placement discussion, you also need to consider airflow through the radiator and engine compartment. If the hood sides are smooth, you need to be sure there's enough room around the engine that the air can move into and then out of the engine compartment.

In the frame chapter, we provided 5 inches as the minimum clearance between the bottom of the oil pan and the ground. Take a look at the better-known cars, and some of the mock-ups seen in this book. The engines look almost too high in the frame, but they're placed that way for a variety of good reasons. By avoiding the tendency to locate the engine too low in the chassis, you sidestep the problem that comes from having the water pump and fan hub too low on the radiator to mount an effective fan.

In a side-to-side sense, the engine needs to be in the center of the frame even if Detroit does sometimes offset the engine slightly to the right. During the mock-up sessions, be sure to spend time considering the engine location—not only for clearance and airflow, but to make sure the steering shaft and possibly the steering box will clear the engine and exhaust.

The Mounts

Nearly all modern engines are mounted to the frame by three engine mounts. The two front mounts handle the bulk of the weight and also handle the enormous torque generated by a modern V-8.

The mounts themselves can be stock factory-style mounts, or something from the aftermarket. Companies like Chassis Engineering manufacture a series of motor mount kits designed to help you install a wide variety of engines into an equally wide variety of frames. Among the stronger and cleaner of the motor mounts currently available for popular engines are the triangulated tubular mounts seen on many hot rods.

We've said it before, if it doesn't cool it isn't worth a damn. Pick your radiator with care—be sure it has enough capacity for your car and accessories. Be sure, too, that the cooling air can get into, and out of, the engine compartment.

Every engine installation should include a good radiator and shroud. A shroud has a dramatic effect on the amount of air moving over the core and the temperature of the coolant.

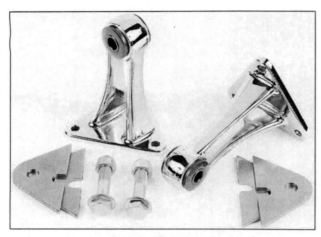

If you want engine mounts that are both strong and sexy, try these cast stainless mounts, complete with tabs to be welded to the frame. *Deuce Factory*

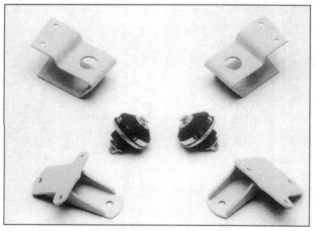

Chassis Engineering makes available kits that ease the installation of nearly any engine into nearly any chassis. The engine, frame brackets, and cushions are sold separately from a large menu. Just mix and match. *Chassis Engineering*

These mounts are very strong and can be purchased as a kit from Deuce Factory or made up from tubing and bushings meant for a four-link kit. In a structural sense, remember that triangles are good, while flat plate welded to the rails to meet the engine, without any supporting members, is not so good.

At SO-CAL, they like to use factory engine mounts. As Shane explains, "The factories spent lots of time designing a mount that doesn't vibrate, so we use theirs. The triangulated ones are sexier, but they only use the little urethane bushing so they transmit more vibration. Our cars are built to drive, and the customers don't like to feel those harmonics."

In terms of the driveline angles, Shane and the crew at SO-CAL follow a time-tested procedure. "Basically we mount the engine with the carb base level, which usually puts the crank at a 2- or 3-degree angle (the tail shaft lower). There's a rule that the pinion angle should be the same as the crank angle, so we rotate the rear end pinion to the same angle."

Mounting the engine and transmission in the frame, especially during the mock-up phase, is made much easier with a small rack to set the engine on. This can be a fairly simple affair, strong enough to hold the engine and transmission up off the table. If you make it a little short, blocks and shims can be used to get the engine and tranny in the perfect position for height and angle. If you don't have a rack as described, you'll be wrestling with an engine dangling on a chain, trying to determine the location of the mounts and how much angle is enough.

A lot of shops use a simple trick to ensure the engine is level from side to side: First they install two bolts in the front of the engine block, through timing cover or water pump holes. Then they run a piece of square tubing across the frame rails, and finally let the engine come down so the bolts touch the tubing (note the photos).

To Shift or Not to Shift

Once you've chosen an engine for the hot rod, you need to pick a transmission. The easy way out is to buy an engine and transmission as a unit. The other easy default setting is to use a TH 350 transmission behind the ever-present small-block.

Up until recently, 99 percent of newly built hot rods came with an automatic transmission. That is no longer the case, in part because many of the bigger builders are incorporating a clutch linkage in their most popular chassis. In fact, both Roy Brizio and SO-CAL have designed clutch linkages that make a manual transmission a viable option.

Linking the Clutch Pedal with the Throw-Out Bearing

Designing and installing the clutch linkage—often the most daunting part of adding a stick shift—is now easier because of the availability of hydraulic clutch linkage assemblies. Instead of trying to figure out the pivot points for the underhood linkage and how to mount a clutch pedal and pivot assembly, you simply need one clutch pedal with a master cylinder, one hydraulic line, and one clutch slave cylinder. The slave cylinder can be mounted to the outside of the bell housing or internally, on the transmission's front bearing retainer. The internal slave cylinders, often called hydraulic throw-out bearings, save space and simplify the linkage, though they require that you pull the transmission if you have to service the slave cylinder assembly.

Complete clutch pedal assemblies with the master cylinder and the pivot mechanism are available from companies like Wilwood. Many American cars and trucks now use hydraulic linkage. If you're installing a Ford engine and transmission, a stock bell housing and slave cylinder plumbed to an aftermarket master cylinder might be the easiest way to proceed.

At SO-CAL, they've designed a longer pedal pivot with room for two pedals instead of just one. The pedals themselves are blanks purchased from the aftermarket and then welded up in the SO-CAL shop. The pivots are sourced from the GM parts catalog, while the cross-shaft is a fabricated piece. For a bell housing, they use a Lakewood unit, modified with the addition of a pivot on the bell housing's left side. The throw-out bearing fork is a Corvette piece.

At Roy Brizio's shop they do it a little differently, but then, the example they provided was for a Ford engine and transmission. Roy explains that when they use a Ford bell housing, they "like to use the Mustang cable system. Inside we use a hot rod clutch pedal and pivot. We attach a heim joint to the upper end of the Mustang cable and use the stock bell housing pivot, arm, and throw-out assembly. It's a nice system and you can throw a spare cable in the trunk just in case."

In building a car with a stick transmission, you don't have to follow either one of these recipes exactly. The point is that the installation of a four- or five-speed transmission is a viable option. An option that, when exercised, will require some modification to the otherwise standard chassis.

The time to figure out the linkage is during the mock-up. At that time you will also need a bell housing and transmission, so you can decide where to put the rear cross-member and mount.

The rear cross-member should be removable. This way the transmission can be removed from under the car, and you won't have to pull the engine just to service the transmission. The rear transmission mount doesn't hold a tremendous amount of weight, and most shops use the factory mount adapted to their own cross-member.

Four, Five, or Six:
Choosing a Standard Transmission

Twenty years ago, it seems there was only one drivetrain in use for 90 percent of the street rods being built. That drivetrain can be abbreviated by three numbers: 350, 350, and 9. The standard engine was a 350 small-block, and behind that sat the standard TH 350 GM automatic transmission. A little farther back was the final member of the drivetrain trio, the 9-inch Ford rear end.

The only part of this scenario that hasn't really changed is the rear end. While there are more

Simple motor-mount brackets like these use factory GM mounts, which means minimal engine vibration transferred to the car. *Deuce Factory*

independent rear ends turning up under modern hot rods, the 9-inch Ford is still the single most popular choice. What has changed is both of the first two numbers in the typical drivetrain description. In fact, there may no longer be a typical, or standard, engine and transmission combination. Engine choices range from flatheads to Hemis, and transmission choices include both slush-boxes and gear-grinding four-, five-, and six-speeds.

For those who want to install a standard transmission behind their big- or small-block, three of the more popular options include an old standard four-speed sourced at the swap meet, a four- or five-speed already attached to the used engine of your choice, or a four-, five-, or six-speed sourced from Richmond Gear Company.

Swap meet transmissions suffer the same caveats as anything else purchased on Sunday morning from unknown suppliers without any warranty intended or implied. Parts for many of the old transmissions are very hard to come by, so unless you know the transmission you're buying is in perfect condition, it can be a risky undertaking.

At SO-CAL, Shane reports that "pretty much all of our cars with sticks use transmissions from Richmond Gear, though we have done a few cars with a Muncie or T-10 transmission." In most cases SO-CAL uses their own clutch linkage, as shown elsewhere in this book, but occasionally they use the hydraulic throw-out bearing assembly on one of the five- or six-speed transmissions from Richmond Gear.

One of the better ways to obtain a transmission that will bolt up to your engine is to buy the engine and transmission as a unit, such as an engine and tranny lifted from a Mustang GT or Camaro. On the plus side of the ledger, consider that you get the correct clutch and flywheel assembly along with the bell housing, and possibly some usable clutch linkage.

Though you can't buy a new Muncie four-speed, you can buy a new Super T-10 from Richmond Gear. As Stewart Hamilton at Richmond Gear explains: "When Borg Warner quit making the Super T-10, Doug Nash bought the rights to the transmission. Then he started manufacturing a five-speed transmission as well. Eventually we bought out Doug Nash, so now we make the Super T-10 and the five-speed. We also added a gear to the five-speed to make our own six-speed transmission."

Stewart reports that the Super T-10 is available "just like they were 20 years ago, or with improved heavy-duty synchronizers and a sturdier tail housing. The heavy-duty version of the Super T-10 was developed for Winston Cup cars and is still used in many of the schools, like the Richard Petty Driving Experience."

Anyone who calls Richmond Gear looking for a transmission to fit their hot rod will first have to answer a series of questions, all designed to ensure that they get exactly the right transmission for their particular situation.

"First, I want to know the weight of the car," explains Stewart. "Next, the tire size, both the diameter and the width. I need to know what powerplant you're using, is it a big-block or a small-block, for example. I need to know what the rear end ratio is and finally, I want to know how the car will be used. On the street or street and strip, and the percentages of each. I need to know if it will be equipped with slicks, in order to get a feel for how much torque you're going to transmit through the drivetrain."

The new heavy-duty Super T-10 is rated at 450 foot-pounds of torque, and that is enough for most street driven cars. "Even if the engine dynos at 600 foot-pounds," explains Stewart, "it's real unlikely you're going to pass all of that torque through the drivetrain."

If the Super T-10 is deemed insufficient for the job, then the tech at Richmond Gear will recommend using a five- or six-speed, either of which will handle much more torque. "If the torque is too high, we move him or her into a five- or six-speed transmission," explains Stewart. "The cost isn't tremendously different between the four- and the five-speed, but the six-speed transmission is quite a bit more money than the five-speed. We want to get enough information from the buyer so the transmission does what they expect it to do. In the old days, the T-10s worked because the tires were skinny and the rubber was hard. Now we've got sticky radial tires and engines that are often more powerful than they were then, so you need a better transmission."

The Richmond gear five-speed uses a one-to-one fifth gear, just like a conventional four-speed, but it has a much lower first gear. "Our first gear is 3.28 to 1," says Stewart, "while first in a four-speed is something like 2.22 to 1. Our low gear is so low it's like having a 4.11 or 4.56 rear end ratio when you take off. They need to run something like a 3.08 rear end with our five-speed. That way when they get into fifth gear the rpms will be the same as with an overdrive."

Stewart feels that most people do fine with a five-speed, that the sexy sixth gear is really only useful for special applications. "It's a rare application where they need a six-speed. The six-speed is good for guys who street and strip the car, or someone who does road-racing. But for most people, *if they gear the rear end correctly*, the five-speed will work just fine."

When I asked about the mistakes people make in choosing a transmission, Stewart reports a lack of planning as the main culprit. "They don't sit down and plan out what they are trying to do ahead of time. If they would spend more time up front thinking, they would be happier, and so would our tech guy."

Shiftless Options and Considerations
Smoking is bad for the health of your transmission

Most automatic transmissions that die premature deaths do so because of excessive heat. Burnouts, drag racing, and trailer towing all generate excessive heat. Without a good cooler, your nice rebuilt transmission could easily die an early death. Most Detroit cars incorporate the transmission cooler into the radiator. The hot rod aftermarket also makes radiators for most cars that have built-in tranny coolers, but it's still a good idea to use a separate cooler. During the mock-up, be sure to plan the installation of a cooler somewhere on the car where there's good airflow. The added benefit of the separate cooler is the fact that it takes one more load off the radiator.

If you buy a used transmission, it's a good idea to have it overhauled before installation. At the very least change the fluid and filter before you fire it up for the first time. When it comes to the clutch in a sealed lock-up torque converter, there's no way to check these sealed units. To ensure the clutch is good, you have to bite the bullet and buy a rebuilt torque converter.

Some Tranny Choices
Ford

Ford Motor Company offers three automatics that often find their way into hot rods. These include the C4, C6, and the newer AOD automatic. The C4 is fine for small-block Ford engines of modest power (the C4 can also be adapted to Ford flatheads with a couple of aftermarket kits), while the C6 is a much stronger transmission. Parts for the C6 are still readily available, despite the transmission's age. Much younger than the C6 is the

AOD, used behind current Ford small-blocks including Mustang GTs. This is a true four-speed transmission, though Ford uses mechanical control of the lock-up torque converter instead of electric control.

GM

Among the many offerings from the General, the Turbo Hydro 350 is still the most popular. This transmission was built from 1969 to 1979 with a standard torque converter, and from 1980 to 1986 in a lock-up version. There are ca-zillions of these transmissions out there in the bone yards and at swap meets. The advantages include the relatively small size, short length, and overall shape, which means this transmission usually fits readily even in frames with the factory X-member. The other big plus here is the ready availability of parts. Earlier, pre-lock-up, transmissions are the more desirable to buy. Most of these TH 350 housings are identical with the exception of some four-by-four housings and reinforced truck housings.

Differences in length from one TH 350 to another are always in the tail-shaft housing. Most of these housings measure either 6 or 9 inches long. The total tranny length with the short housing is just over 28 inches from the edge of the bell housing to the end of the tail-shaft housing. The rear mount bolts to the main transmission case, not the tail-shaft housing. This is a good thing, as the location of the rear mount is not affected by your choice of tail-shaft housings.

Another difference to watch for is in the diameter of the speedometer drive housings. Chevrolet trannys used a speedo housing that was about 1 inch in diameter, while most of those used in Buicks, Oldsmobiles, and Pontiacs have a much larger hole and speedometer-gear housing. The installation of a TH 350 will require a shift linkage, a vacuum line to the transmission's modulator, and a kick-down cable.

The heavy-duty member of the older GM line is the Turbo Hydro 400. This transmission was installed behind many high-horsepower engines and GM trucks. Installing a TH400 might be more work, as these units are somewhat heavier and longer by 1 inch than a TH 350. They are also slightly larger in diameter and wider across the rear, which may interfere with some X-members. The hot rodder with a very heavy foot or a heavy car might do well to consider the TH400. Again, you need shift linkage and a vacuum line to the vacuum modulator. In place of a kick-down cable, the 400 uses a throttle-activated electric switch to downshift for passing.

You may have heard of the switch-pitch TH400, used only from 1965 to 1967. This transmission used a stator (the vaned unit positioned between the drive and driven members of the torque converter) with pivoting vanes. The angle of the vanes could be changed from a *high stall speed* for acceleration to a *low stall speed* for efficient highway cruising. These units make a good street rod transmission, though they might be hard to find. If you're interested, check with a specialty automatic transmission shop.

Overdrive transmissions from the GM line include the well-known 700 R4, a real four-speed transmission with a lock-up torque converter. The 700 R4 gives you a low first-gear ratio, 3.06:1, and an overdrive fourth gear, 0.70:1. You can have your cake and eat it too: a good hole shot and low revs on the highway.

A good 700 R4 can handle substantial amounts of torque and horsepower. These transmissions come with two bell-housing bolt patterns: the 2.8 V-6 and four-cylinder cars used a bell housing with a slightly different (*metric*) bolt pattern, while trannies for the 4.3 V-6 and all small-blocks have what most of us would consider the correct bolt pattern. The two upper mounting holes measure 8.25 inches from center to center on the "right" transmission.

Units assembled after 1987 are superior to earlier units (later trannies have pressure ports on the side next to the servo, while the earlier models do not). The earliest 700 R4s can be upgraded with the latest parts, however.

GM introduced a lighter-duty overdrive transmission, the 200 4R, in the early 1980s. Not to be confused with a modified 350, these are totally separate from the 700 R4 transmissions. A perfectly good, four-speed transmission, the 200 4R provides many of the advantages of the 700 R4 in a small, less expensive package. The smaller size of the 200

Though the Turbo 350 transmission from GM might seem an antique, it has one very nice attribute—it fits fairly easily into a Ford frame with an X-member.

137

4R means it often fits a fat-Ford frame with little or no modification of the X-member.

Mopar

The best known of the Chrysler transmissions is the venerable Torqueflite, a design that was produced in two versions, the 904 and the 727. The bigger 727 is certainly the best unit from the perspective of strength. However, a 904 will work just fine with small-blocks of reasonable power. Physically the two transmissions are very close to the same size, though the 727 is a bit meatier through the center of the housing. The big Torqueflite can be built to Hemi specs and beyond. There are also two overdrive versions of the Torqueflite, the A500 and A518, which correspond to the 904 and 727 respectively.

Final Transmission Notes

If you can't decide or aren't sure which automatic transmission to run, it's a good idea to call up and speak with an expert. Greg Ducato from Phoenix Transmission Products in Phoenix suggests that the potential builder have a really good understanding of what he or she wants from the car and base their decisions accordingly. Do they intend to race the car or just cruise to weekend events? Greg also feels that people don't think enough about the rear end ratio. "If you have a 2.7 or 3.0:1 rear end and lots of power, you don't need an overdrive. But if the car has a 4:11:1 gear you don't need a 350 or 400 transmission. If you install the 350 or 400 with the 4:11 gears, then you can't drive it any distance because the engine is spinning so fast on the highway."

Mounting the Rear End

Rear end choices are covered pretty well in the rear suspension chapter. At this point it is worth repeating Shane's comments that at SO-CAL they generally install the engine and transmission at a 2- or 3-degree angle (with the tail-shaft lower) and the rear end at the same angle. It's also worth noting that many of these rear suspensions allow the user to alter the pinion angle once the rear end housing is installed. This doesn't mean you don't have to be careful about welding the brackets on, you do. But often there is a bit of adjustment left if you decide your initial estimate was off slightly, or you feel the need to try a slightly different pinion angle.

When you look at most chassis in the top view, the rear end has an offset to one side—the U-joint yoke is not exactly centered between the two backing plates. Seen from above, the center-line of the pinion and the engine are usually offset slightly, though the two centerlines are parallel. Most builders leave this offset intact so the finished, narrowed rear end housing will position the driveshaft in the center of the driveshaft tunnel. Shane adds that, "Some people might want the rear end 'centered' for appearance reasons."

Before welding on the suspension brackets, the rear end should be mocked up in the chassis with everything at ride height. The brackets should be welded on to the housing before any narrowing work is finished. The idea is to have all the welding that will cause warpage done before the housing ends are final-welded in place. The housing ends themselves should be welded in place by an experienced shop that uses a fixture to keep the housing straight and true.

No matter how careful the shop is when they weld on the ends, the housing may still become warped and need to be sent out to a shop like Currie's to be straightened.

Rear End Choices

The overwhelming choice when it comes to solid axle rear ends is the Ford 9-inch housing and center section. There are alternatives, and they include everything from the smaller, 8-inch Ford rear end to the venerable quick-change.

The big 9-inch Ford rear ends are popular for a number of reasons. First, the rear end is very durable and will easily withstand the abuse dished out by a typical hot rodder. Even nostalgia drag-racers will find the Ford rear end more than able to make pass after pass down the strip. And because of their popularity, a large variety of aftermarket parts are available for the 9-inch, including complete ultra heavy-duty third-members.

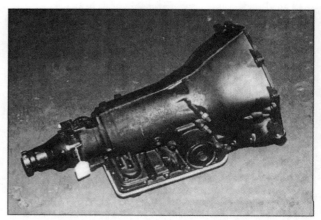

When deciding which transmission to run you need to consider more than just cost and gearing. Though the R4 shown here makes a great overdrive transmission, the right side of the case often interferes with the frame's X-member. The 200 4R, though not as heavy-duty, is an overdrive transmission that often fits more easily in many street rod frames.

Despite its popularity with drag-racers, hot rodders, and off roaders, the 9-inch Ford rear end is still available from most used parts emporiums or at the Sunday swap meet. As the hobby matures, more and more parts become available as complete units, ready to install, and this is certainly true of 9-inch rear ends. If you elect to let your fingers do the walking, companies like Currie Enterprises will provide you with a complete 9-inch assembly, including a new "smooth" center housing, narrowed to meet your specifications. You can have any bolt pattern you need to match up with the front axle, and either disc or drum brakes already installed.

For hands-on rodders who like to walk between the rows of rusty cars stacked three high looking for just the right parts, there is more than one style of Ford 9-inch rear end. First, understand that the 9-inch was used in passenger cars from 1957 to 1973, in pickup trucks until 1984, and in full-size vans all the way to 1987. Factory 9-inch rear ends come in various widths, with different diameter axles and different numbers of splines on the end.

One of the things that makes the 9-inch a good choice is the fact that the area just behind the axle splines with the reduced diameter is short. This makes it more likely that after the axle is cut, the new axle-end will be the full diameter so it can be re-splined. The factory axles come in two diameters, with either 28 or 31 splines.

The larger-diameter axle can be either 28 or 31 splines, while the smaller diameter is always a 28-spline axle. Larger-diameter axles come with larger-diameter wheel bearings mounted in larger-diameter axle housings. The hot ticket for hot rod use is a long housing from a pickup truck or a station wagon (so the axles are longer) with the larger-diameter housing. If you can find a used one with the positraction, that makes it that much more desirable.

We suggest buying a wide housing because in most cases you have to narrow the rear end anyway, and with longer axles it's more likely that shortening the axle will remove enough material to get past the small-diameter area behind the splines.

There are some Lincoln Versailles and Granada rear ends that measure about 58 inches flange to flange and may work in some fat-fendered street rods. Some of these have the added advantage of factory disc brakes. Most, however, will need to be narrowed, so you might just as well get one as wide as you can.

Ford also made an 8-inch rear end. Though not as bulletproof as a 9-inch, this is a perfectly suitable rear end for the street rodder with a milder engine under the hood or a lighter foot. Though they typi-cally cost less than a 9-inch and are a third-member design, the 8-inch Ford isn't available in as many gear ratios and is becoming hard to find.

Also available from the blue-oval folks is an 8.8-inch rear end. These come standard in Mustang GTs and may be available in the junkyards. Ford SVO also sells the 8.8 new through their catalog with gear sets as deep as 4.10:1. In addition, SVO offers complete 9-inch housings with the large-diameter bearing retainers narrow enough to fit the Mustang bodies, another possible source for 9-inch housings that don't need narrowing.

At SO-CAL, they start with raw 9-inch Ford rear end housings and put them in a jig before the brackets can be installed.

Other options in the rear end department include the 12-bolt GM housing, though these are not third-member-type rear ends; this makes it harder for the typical street rodder to service the rear end or change gear ratios.

The Chrysler 8 3/4-inch rear ends are very durable and may work well for the Mopar fanatic. Readily available in the junkyard, these rear ends are another third-member design. If you can find one from a Dodge Dart or Duster, it might even be close enough for use without narrowing. If you can't find a narrow enough rear end, though, you will likely have to buy new axles, as the Mopar axles tend to have a lengthy small-diameter area behind the splines.

Some Mopars, like the Street Hemis from the wild and crazy '60s, ran the Dana 44 or Dana 60 rear end. These heavy-duty rear ends are still available in the aftermarket. Though very durable, both these rear ends are non-third-member designs and are seldom seen on street rods.

The best reason to use a 9-inch is similar to the reasons people often cite for running a small-block Chevy engine: Because the 9-inch is so common, parts and service are easy to come by and relatively inexpensive. Sometimes it pays, literally, to run the same equipment as everyone else.

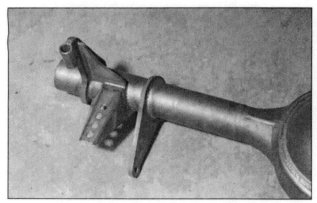

After the four-bar and shock brackets are installed, the rear end goes to Currie Enterprises for installation of the ends and any necessary straightening.

The popularity of the 9-inch rear end means that complete heavy-duty center sections are available brand-new.

What About a Quick-Change?

When it comes to rear ends, no name has quite the ring that Halibrand does. Early hot rodders borrowed ideas and components from race cars of the period to enhance both the performance and the perceived performance of their street machines. Designed for sprint cars, a Halibrand rear end installed in your Model A or Deuce roadster made for a machine that was both hot and cool at the same time.

Richard LeJuerrne, current owner of Halibrand, explains that the earliest blueprint they can find for a quick-change rear end carries a date of 1948, *though* the company was formed one year earlier. "After the war Ted Halibrand built products simply to improve the performance of his own race cars. He started with the mag wheels and then invented the quick-change rear end later. Hot rodders adopted his parts, as soon as a supply became available from old race cars."

Ted Halibrand was a great designer, though he never could see the aftermarket. To him these were

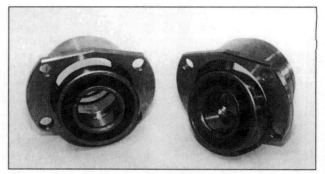

Billet steel axle-housing ends are available for narrowed rear ends, in both a small- and a large-bearing model.

race-car parts, period. Today, Halibrand still makes two versions of the original rear end, the Champ and the V-8 rear end. Unlike in Ted's day, however, Halibrand now sells components both to race car and street rod builders. And though it's hard to tell an old Halibrand from a new one, they have changed over the years. "We have upgraded the rear ends for better sealing," explains Richard, "and we added positraction and so on. But some of these castings come from the same sand patterns first used after the war. We're about to finish the third generation of independent rear end assemblies utilizing the original center sections. All of this *allows* us to offer more products that fit a wider range of possible applications."

Though they might be the coolest rear ends on the street, most hot rodders see three reasons not to install a Halibrand: price, clearance, and noise. "Our rear ends do cost more than a complete 9-inch Ford," admits Richard, "but not by as much as you would think. The difference might only be $400 when you compare ours to a complete assembly you buy from one of the companies advertising in *Street*

Whether or not a quick-change is extra work to install depends on the chassis. In the case of this Deuce seen in the SO-CAL shop, the frame needs the correct rear cross-member, and a notch in the gas tank.

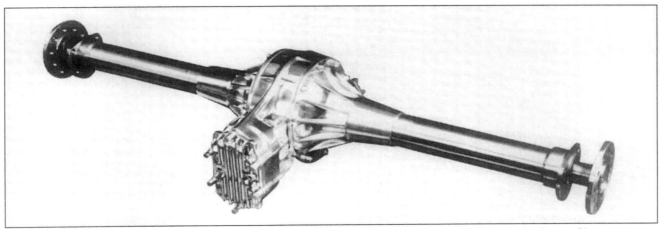

What we think of as a "quick-change" rear end actually comes in two versions from Halibrand: the larger Champ rear end, and the V-8 assembly, shown here. The V-8 quick-change uses a ring gear 8.8 inches in diameter. The quick-change gears mean you can have your choice of gear ratios all the way from 7.95:1 to 1.80:1. The complete rear end comes in 55- and 57-inch widths, flange to flange. It can also be combined with early-Ford axle housings to make a complete nostalgia package. *Halibrand*

Rodder. And the clearance issue depends on the car. I have one in my '32 Ford, which meant I had to notch the rear cross-member. In my '39 Ford it wasn't a problem, I used a Pete and Jake's cross-member and there's no clearance problem at all."

As for the noise issue (a whine caused by straight-cut gears), Richard reports that, "We have helical-cut gears available for both rear ends, and they eliminate 95 percent of the noise. There's still a whine, but you hear that in a new '40 Ford rear end as well just because of the design."

In terms of strength, the V-8 rear end uses an 8.8-inch ring gear that Richard reports is,

"comparable in strength to a 9-inch Ford ring gear. But when you start to see 450 horsepower and above, then it's time to step up to the Champ rear end. Surprisingly, the limiting factor in terms of strength is the quick-change gears, not the ring and pinion."

The more substantial Champ assembly uses a ring gear nearly 10 inches in diameter and is available with a Detroit Locker limited-slip differential. Both rear ends come with 31-spline axles in 55- and 57-inch widths and can be ordered with a variety of Wilwood rear disc brake calipers and rotors.

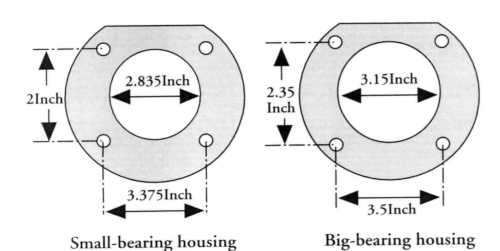

Small-bearing housing   Big-bearing housing

Take this sketch along when you go to the swap meet to make sure that "big bearing" 9-inch housing really is as advertised.

The installation of the clutch linkage starts with the installation of the engine, Lakewood bell housing, and six-speed transmission.

Greg Petersen sets the engine down on factory mounts, both in the front and the rear.

This short mock-up sequence shows how a typical engine is set up and installed at the SO-CAL shop. Also shown here is the assembly of the mechanical clutch linkage. The frame is a typical SO-CAL frame except that the main cross-member is positioned 1 1/4 inches farther back to make room for a six-speed transmission from Richmond Gear. Because of this change, the ladder bars have been shortened 1 inch to match the new position of the cross-member. The other difference is in the bar that supports the master cylinder. This frame is designed for a standard transmission, so this one tube has a different angle than it would if the frame were meant for an automatic transmission.

Greg Petersen starts the installation by first mating the engine block, with the Lakewood bell housing attached, to the Richmond Gear six-speed transmission. Once the engine and transmission are united as a unit and well balanced on the engine hoist, Greg slides the assembly into place. We should note that the engine has the factory-style mounts already attached, and they mate up with the SO-CAL motor mounts, already welded to the frame in their standard location.

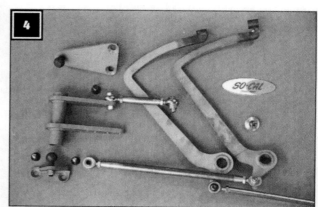

The parts that make up the SO-CAL clutch linkage are sourced from the local GM dealer, the hot rod aftermarket, and the SO-CAL shop.

An electronic level gauge is a handy tool and a good way to ensure the frame is sitting at ride height—a necessary first step in checking the angle of the engine.

Here you can see the inner mount bolted to bungs welded to the bell housing, and the outer mount bolted to the frame rail.

Because the mounts are already in position, Greg knows that the engine is sitting in the frame at an angle of about 2 degrees. The next project is the assembly of the clutch linkage.

At the heart of this linkage is the cross-shaft, a piece fabricated at the SO-CAL shop. Greg starts by bolting the inner pivot to the bungs already welded to the bell housing. Next, he slides the cross-shaft in place and then attaches the outer pivot to the left frame rail. Though not shown here, the cross-shaft will be equipped with a grease zerk for periodic lubrication.

The two pedals are both made up in the SO-CAL shop from blanks, and slide on to the extra-long pivot shaft already installed in the frame. With the rods supplied as part of the SO-CAL clutch linkage kit, Greg is able to attach the clutch pedal to the cross-shaft, and then the cross-shaft to the clutch arm. The master cylinder pushrod attaches directly to the bottom of the brake pedal and runs straight back to the dual-chamber master cylinder.

Both the clutch and the brake linkage are simple mechanical connections that should serve for a long, long time without the need for maintenance or repair.

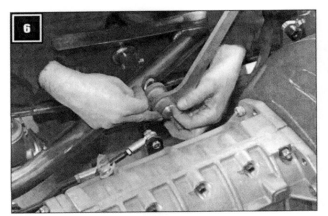

The double pedals are mounted on the extra-long pivot shaft and held in place with a bolt that screws into the end on the shaft.

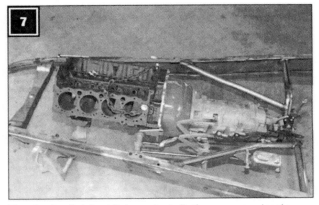

Here's the finished linkage installation—neat, simple, and pretty much foolproof.

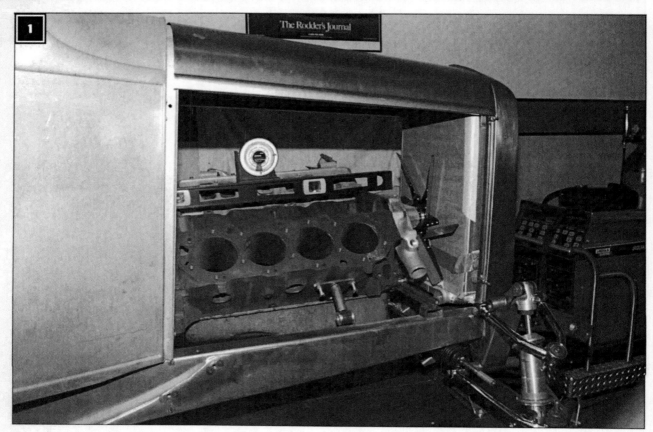

As mentioned in chapter 2, part of the mock-up session was spent trying to determine where the engine would have to be positioned in order to allow room for a big, belt-driven fan.

Like most parts of building a hot rod, installation of the drivetrain in the stretched Deuce pickup didn't happen all at once. The sequences that follow were often separated by weeks, while Neal waited for parts or took time to do another part of the building and fabrication process.

Installing the Engine and Transmission

The engine and transmission are installed the first time as part of the first mock-up. The TH400 transmission case is bolted to the Chevy big-block, a water pump and fan are added at the front, and the whole affair is set in place. For this first mock-up session, the engine is supported at the front by two 3/8 bolts screwed in to the front of the block, resting on square tubing run across from one frame rail to another. The back of the engine is held up by a small hydraulic floor jack.

This simple system makes it easy to change the angle of the engine by adding or deleting spacers under the tubing at the front of the engine. The front mounts are bolted to the engine, though the tabs on the frame are not yet welded in place.

Though some builders prefer to use the factory mounts because they do a better job of absorbing vibration, Neal and John have chosen to use the small triangular mounts with a simple urethane bushing.

You can buy mounts like these from a variety of sources, but Neal chose to make the mounts seen here. He explains that the mounts are made from readily available components: "It's all standard four-bar parts. Most of it is four-bar tubing, DOM mild steel, 0.875 inches in diameter and 0.156-inch wall thickness. The sleeve is 1.375 inches in diameter, which takes a standard four-bar urethane bushing. I cut the plate from quarter-inch, cold-rolled mild steel. For a lot of hot rod builders this is all stuff they've already got in stock." Neal much prefers these mounts to those used by the

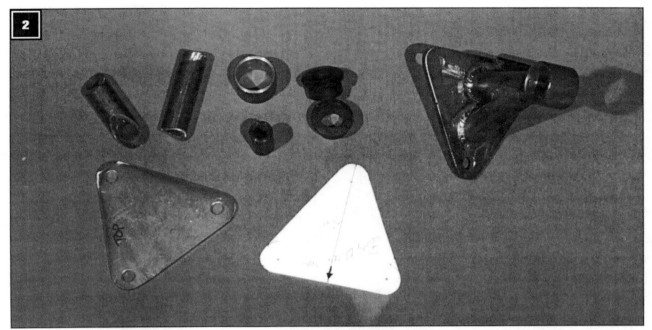

The motor mounts are made in Neal's shop from readily available components: four-bar tubing and cold-rolled mild steel.

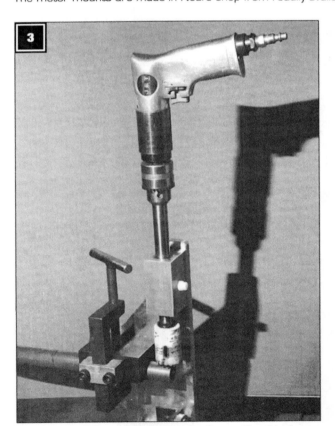

With an air-drill, a hole saw, and a fixture like this from JD Squared, you can cut a nice neat notch on tubing.

factory "because this is a much neater design, a lot cleaner than a GM mount. And a lot stronger too."

As mentioned earlier, Neal and John set the engine and transmission in place and then mocked up the body to see how everything fit. Based on those calculations they decided to move the engine back 1 inch farther in order to provide room behind the radiator for a big, belt-driven fan.

Neal uses a straight edge, placed across the engine from front to rear, and a protractor to check the angle of the engine (more later).

The next time the engine is lowered in place, Neal knows where the engine should be set relative to the radiator and the cowl. At this time he moves the engine to the correct position and then tack-welds the engine-mount tabs to the frame. At the rear of the transmission, Neal uses a factory transmission mount.

The three mounts locate the engine at an angle of 2 degrees, with the rear of the engine lower than the front. The engine is centered in the frame between the two rails, high enough to provide 5 inches of clearance between the bottom of the oil pan and the ground, and to put the fan in the center of the radiator.

When it comes to determining the U-joint and pinion angles, Neal likes to work with a drive shaft in place. "We mocked up a drive shaft from 3-inch-diameter tubing. It slides over the transmission tail-shaft then slides back to where the U-joint yoke would be. Then I measure the angle of the drive

145

Though they transmit more vibration, these mounts can't be beat for their nice clean design and very high strength.

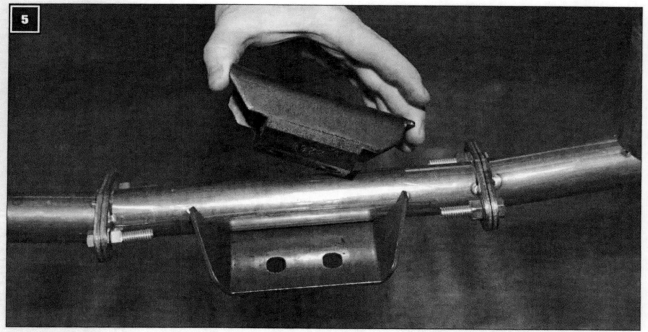

The rear-mounting tab is from Deuce Factory, designed to interface with the standard GM rear engine mount.

Not everyone agrees on the best driveline angles. Neal installs this big-block at 2 degrees from horizontal, with the rear of the engine slightly lower than the front.

shaft and subtract 1 degree to determine my ideal pinion angle. If the drive shaft is at 1 degree from horizontal, for example, the pinion-shaft angle would be at 0. With the three-link suspension, the pinion angle never changes. The whole idea is to load the U-joints slightly, so they "work" as the shaft spins; otherwise the needle bearings don't rotate in the cups and they wear out much faster."

Once Neal knows what he wants for a pinion angle, it's a simple matter of positioning the rear end at that angle (in the brackets Neal made for just such a task) and then mocking up the three-bar linkage. About welding the brackets on the housing, Neal feels it's "impossible to avoid warping the housing." Some minor warpage can be corrected for when the ends are cut off and then re-installed as part of the narrowing process. Any serious warpage, however, will require that the housing be straightened by a shop with a huge hydraulic press and the personnel who understand how to use the press and a set of V-blocks to correct for the effects of too much heat.

With a mock-up drive shaft in place and the rear end housing sitting on stands, it's easy to rotate the housing until there's a difference of about 1 degree between the drive shaft and the pinion.

Chapter 9

Wheels and Tires

As stated again and again in this book, the wheels you choose for your new hot rod are as important as any other part. Pete Chapouris states emphatically that wheels and tires "make the car." More than style is at stake here. Your choice of wheels and tires will help determine how the car handles, turns, and stops. Buying the right wheels means you need to know what will bolt onto the hub, what will fit under the fenders, and what will clear the brake caliper or drum on the backside.

Such an important part of the automotive puzzle needs careful consideration before the final choice is made. Before making a decision, it might help to understand the various types of wheels currently on the market.

Cast or Billet? One Piece or Two?

Most of the wheels that most of us covet are made from aluminum. Why aluminum? Because it's durable, light, easily cast, easily machined, and polishes readily. Most aluminum wheels are either cast or carved from billet. The differences aren't as obvious as they might seem, and some wheels fall into a gray area between the two types.

A fairly traditional roadster needs traditional cast wheels with tall tires. Like Pete says, "The wheels make the car."

Some cars, and even trucks, like this Hemi-powered F100, need nothing more than steel wheels wide enough to mount a decent set of tires. Just paint 'em to match the body and add center caps with beauty rings.

And some early cars, like this unique SO-CAL creation, call for nothing fancier than a set of original "wires."

Billet wheels come in every style, size, and shape imaginable. Designs run the gamut from traditional to very modern. *Budnik*

By forging the center section into a dished shape before the cutting starts, Budnik is able to make a wheel like this in less time and with less waste. *Budnik*

The Famosa is one of the more traditional looking wheels currently available in billet aluminum. *Budnik*

Shaped like an early cast wheel, the Muroc is another two-piece billet wheel available in a wide variety of sizes. *Budnik*

A true billet wheel uses a center section machined from a solid piece (or "billet") of aluminum. These wheels are often described as being made from "6061-T6." The number *6061* describes the alloy of aluminum, while the *T6* describes the heat treatment.

Most billet wheels start as a blank of aluminum. Some companies buy these blanks already cut into circles of the correct diameter, so they need only to be machined and mated with the rim. Other wheel manufacturers buy the aluminum in large sheets and do the "cookie cutting" themselves.

Up until recently, most billet wheel manufacturers ran the blanks through a series of CNC (Computer-Numeric Control) milling machines where the designs, and holes for wheel studs, were milled and drilled into the raw piece of aluminum. In an effort to reduce the huge piles of waste aluminum generated *every day*, at least one billet wheel manufacturer currently forms the blank with forging dies before the machining starts.

After machining, the center section is mated to an already formed aluminum rim, making this a two-piece wheel. The center sections are designed to have a slight interference fit relative to the rim. First the center sections are pressed in place and positioned for the correct back spacing.

Next comes a check for runout, and then the center section and rim are joined with a bead welded all along the back side.

The beauty of the billet wheel lies in the infinite number of designs that can be used on the center section, combined with the high strength of the 6061 alloy. As the CNC lathes and mills become more advanced, the designs get more and more complex. Tapered and fluted designs that would have required careful handwork (if they could be done at all) a few years back can now be programmed into the computers that run the machines. The result is some truly outstanding designs.

Cast Wheels

A cast wheel is just that, cast. To oversimplify, molten aluminum is poured into a mold and allowed to cool. Once cool the wheel can be pulled out of the mold, cleaned up, and sent to the polishing shop.

Cast wheels generally include the rim as part of the casting, making this a one-piece wheel. Just to keep things interesting, a cast center section can also be combined with an already-formed rim to create a two-piece wheel, much the way most billet wheels are assembled. And just because the wheel is cast with the concave face and the slots already in place doesn't mean the wheel doesn't get machined (they do) after the casting.

The nature of the casting process dictates that a cast wheel is a less complex design. Generally, casting doesn't allow for the fine, intricate detail seen on billet wheels. Those details can be added after the casting process, but usually aren't.

Cast wheels have their own look, a "softer" look with more gentle curves and fewer angles. Perhaps the best known of the cast wheels is the Halibrand. Part of the nostalgia wave currently in vogue includes a new-found fondness for cast wheels, including the Halibrand and similar designs. The softer shapes seen in a cast wheel are definitely part of a time gone by, a time when a little extra metal was no bad thing.

In reality the casting process is a little more involved. First there's the question of the alloy. Most cast wheels are made from 356 aluminum. Of course not all 356 is created equal. An "A" prefix, for example, designates a higher quality alloy, one with less variance in the alloy specifications.

The casting process is a bit of a black art. We've all heard the term, "sand cast," but few of us understand the intricacies of actually making the mold in the sand. The questions that arise include which type of sand to use and how to avoid porosity problems in the finished wheels. Porosity is enough of a problem that some cast wheels are not rated as tubeless.

Because most of these wheels are cast in one piece, making a wheel with various back spacings is more difficult than it is with a two-piece wheel.

Cast wheels like these seen at PS Engineering get at least three separate quality checks before being shipped to the customer.

Though we think of billet wheels as being two-piece designs, these two-piece wheels use a cast center. This type of wheel makes it easier to provide a wide range of backspacing simply by changing the position of the center relative to the rim.

Changes can sometimes be made by machining off more or less of the material on the inside of the wheel where it mates up against the brake drum or rotor. That process can only be taken so far, of course, meaning that significant changes in back spacing require a different casting altogether, which requires more work and more inventory for the manufacturer.

When it comes to building *your new hot rod*, the importance of the wheels and tires can't be

Halibrand calls this traditional wheel the Speedway spindle mount. It's designed to leave room for disc brakes on the back side. *Halibrand*

Phil Schmidt started his wheel company with little more than a background in engineering and an interest in vintage race cars. The combination must work; today PS Engineering manufactures both one- and two-piece cast wheels in a variety of designs and sizes.

At PS Engineering, the wheel lathe is used to clean up the castings and ensure there is essentially no runout.

A mix of old and new, this Halibrand Sweet Swirl puts a twist (literally) on the traditional cast wheel. *Halibrand*

Two very similar tires, likely to have very different effects when driven in the rain. Note how the siping on the left-hand tire is designed to help the water exit from under the tire, while the tire on the right is likely to trap that same water.

overstated. The wheels are what you build the car around, so whether they're cast, billet, steelies, or wires, give the decision plenty of thought.

The Wheel Lexicon

To describe a wheel, any wheel, requires a few technical terms like *bolt circle* and *offset*. A definition of each term follows.
• The *bolt circle* is the diameter of the bolt circle, preceded by the number of lugs. For example, 4x4.5 means the rim has four bolt holes and that the diameter of the bolt circle is 4 1/2 inches.
You can figure the bolt circle diameter on a wheel with five studs with a simple formula. You only need to know the distance between two adjacent studs (the centerline distance) and then multiply that figure by a constant (1.7013).
• The *hub diameter* is the diameter of the hole in the center of the wheel.
• The *rim width* is the distance across the rim, measured on the inside of the rim flange.
• The *wheel back spacing* is the distance between the wheel's mounting surface and the rim's inside flange.
• The *wheel front spacing* is the distance from the wheel mounting surface to the rim's outer flange.
• The *offset* is where this gets confusing. Offset is

a measure of how far *offset* the center of the rim is from the wheel mounting surface. A chrome reverse rim is one with the offset to the outside. Modern front-wheel-drive cars often exhibit offset to the inside. Trying to decide if offset to the outside of the car should be referred to as positive or negative depends on who you ask, so we won't use the terms at all here.
• The *wheel load capacity* refers to the amount of weight the wheel can safely withstand.
When buying a set of wheels you also need to consider the type of lug nut required by a particular rim. Also keep in mind that disc brake calipers sometimes hit the back side of certain rims and that the big-finned Buick brake drums likewise need extra clearance on the backside of the rim.

Tires

Like wheels, describing a tire requires the use of certain technical terms.

The *aspect ratio* (or how "tall" a tire is) can be described as the section height divided by the section width. The smaller the number the "wider" the tire, relative to its height. A 205/50R15 is a 15-inch tire *with an aspect ratio of 50. This tire is 50 percent* as high as it is wide. A

205/75R15 is a 15-inch tire with an aspect ratio of 75; this tire is 75 percent as high as it is wide. In the BFGoodrich line, their All-Terrain P205/75R15 is 27.3 inches in total diameter and 6 inches wide, while in their Comp T/A line, the 205/50ZR15 is 23.1 inches in total diameter and 6.2 inches wide.

The sidewall of nearly any tire is marked with a confusing array of numbers and letters embossed into the rubber. Among all those numbers and codes is the speed rating, a letter code that indicates the highest sustained speed the tire is designed to withstand.

Code	Top Speed
N	87 mph
P	93 mph
Q	99 mph
R	106 mph
S	113 mph
T	118 mph
H	130 mph
V	149 mph
Z	Speeds in excess of 149 mph

The speed rating can be integrated into the tire size. P205/60SR15, for example, can be interpreted as follows: the *P* indicates passenger car use, the *S* is the speed rating (up to 113 mph), and the *R* simply indicates that the tire is a radial.

When buying tires, you have to keep a few more things in mind, like the relationship between rim width and tire size. If you try to put too wide a tire on a particular rim, the tire's tread will never flatten out when it's on the car. Tire manufacturers provide charts that provide the recommended rim width for a certain tire. You can only vary so far from the recommended rim widths. Often a good tire salesperson can provide some real-world advice as to how much rim you need for a certain tire. Remember, too, that the ultimate width of an installed and inflated tire is affected by the rim width. The wider the rim the wider the tire profile (you can only go so far with this of course). If you're in doubt about the right combination of rim and tire, ask to see the published recommendations for your new tires.

Each manufacturer makes available a chart of specifications. Listed is the diameter and the width of the tread. Also listed is the "section width" and how that width changes as the rim width changes.

There is also a situation known as the "plus fitments." A plus 1 fitment is a way of going from a 14- to a 15-inch tire with the same overall diameter. A P205/70SR14 is the same diameter as a P215/60R15 in one particular brand of tire. The difference is in the sidewall dimension. The 15-inch tire has a much shorter sidewall, which has a major impact both on how the tire looks and on how the car rides and handles.

The Effect of Tire Size

Most hot rods run some pretty big tires on the rear. Highboys in particular run tires that are not only wide, but tall as well. When you've chosen the tire you want from the perspective of looks and final rake, remember to consider the effect of the tire diameter on the car's final gearing. Going from a "standard automotive tire" to one of the tall tires often used on highboys and similar hot rods can make a deep 4:10 to 1 rear end seem like someone

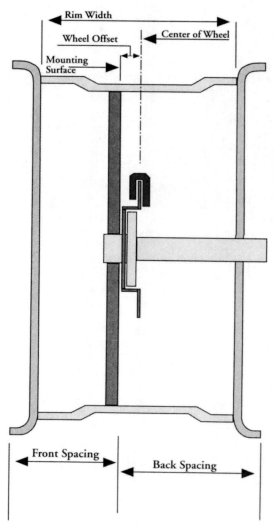

The wheel mounting surface *seldom* ends up in exactly the middle of the rim; thus, most wheels have some offset one way or the other. Remember that there needs to be enough room on the inside of the rim to clear the brake drum or caliper. When planning a car, the chassis manufacturer can offer guidance in picking an ideal wheel. If the car is already built, a good wheel manufacturer can tell you how to measure to get the right amount of offset.

slipped in an overdrive unit. All of this will also be affected by the type of car you're building, how much highway cruising (or drag racing) you intend to do, and the choice of a transmission. Be sure to check out the tire diameter/RPM chart seen in this chapter before making the final decision on your rear end ratio, transmission, and rear tire size.

Nothing says "hot rod" in quite the same way as a set of really wide rear tires. The only downside to that drag-race look is the fact that fat tires tend to hydroplane more easily than a tire with a narrower footprint. It's simply a matter of physics; the wider the tire the farther the water needs to travel to get out from under that footprint. Slicks are illegal on the street for good reason, they're very dangerous in wet conditions. If you want to race, buy the slicks and put them on a separate set of rims. BFGoodrich makes a Comp T/A Drag Radial that combines a sticky compound with minimal siping to keep the tires street legal. While they may be legal for driving to and from the strip, you probably don't want to run these full time.

As Harvey at the Paul Williams Tire Center in Minneapolis states, "When you're looking at wide tires, you need one that moves the water away from the center of the tire. Something with big channels in the center so the water can't build up under the tire." At Paul Williams they point out that you need large enough sipes at the very edge of the tire so the water can actually exit from under the tread. The better tires are designed to channel or pump water from under the tire through the various channels and sipes and thus minimize any build-up of water under the tire.

Some tires that are rated All Weather or even Mud and Snow, don't do an especially good job as a rain tire. Before buying tires, spend time reading the manufacturer's charts and recommendations and talking with knowledgeable people at the tire store.

If tires that are too big pose a potential problem, the other extreme can be just as bad. The big-'n-little look might be great, as long as the little part of the equation isn't taken too far. Among the data printed for each tire is a recommended load limit. The point is that those little tires in front might look really cool, but they do most of the stopping on a hard brake application and they do all the turning. Don't compromise the safety or handling of the car just to be cool.

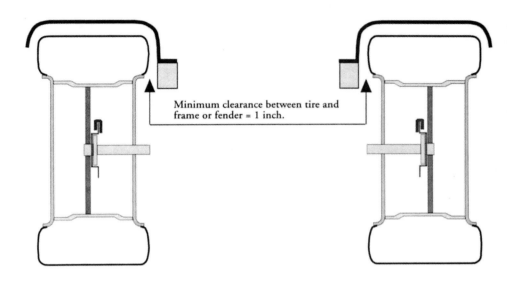

Minimum clearance between tire and frame or fender = 1 inch.

Because the body, frame, and chassis members all move as you drive, there must be at least 1 inch of clearance between the frame, or fender lips, and your tires.

A variety of schemes and formulas have been contrived over the years, all intended to help you determine the right rim with the right offset for that new or existing car. As Pete Chapouris explains, however, the best way to be really sure you get the right tire and wheel combination for the car is to mock up the car at ride height and stick what you think are the right tires and rims under the fenders, assuming there are any fenders. Instead of using a calculator, Pete would rather have you use a tape measure. During the mock-up, be sure to move the suspension up-and-down, and turn the front wheels from lock to lock.

When measuring there are a few things to keep in mind. First, on the rear end you need at least 1 inch of clearance between the side of the tire and the frame rail or fender lip. This minimum clearance must be considered during the building process because car bodies move from side to side as the car moves up-and-down on the suspension. Panhard rods tend to jack the frame slightly from side to side as the suspension moves up-and-down. Rubber bushings often have enough give that the axle housing will move over just a little bit.

It is often better to buy an axle with the right dimension, or to have the rear end narrowed to fit, instead of centering the tire under the fender with an unusual offset. That way you can use relatively standard rims without a lot of extra offset. In the case of a somewhat standard hot rod, don't be afraid to ask around. If the frame is from SO-CAL or TCI, call and ask them for a recommendation on axle width, rim offset, and tire size, before pulling your hair out trying to decide how big a tire to run and how much offset the rim should have.

Alan Budnik, namesake of the huge Budnik Wheels operation, started his career as a machinist. On the way from machinist to well-known wheel manufacturer, Alan worked with some significant characters in the hot rod industry, including Jack Chisenhall, owner of Vintage Air, and Boyd Coddington. Doing this short interview was made especially difficult because Alan had to divide his time between the wheel operation and the construction of a new building in Huntington Beach, California.

Q. Alan, let's start with some background. How did you get started manufacturing wheels, what's your background?

A. I started out as a machinist, working at a local machine shop. First it was manual machines, and then I learned how to do the programming on the CNC machines. I worked with Jack Chisenhall, owner of Vintage Air, on some of his projects. About that time I met some people like Jamie Musselman, who owned some Boyd Coddington cars, and I ended up working with Boyd at the very beginning of his wheel operation. I helped him buy his first CNC machine. After two years I split off from Boyd and had my own shop. I was doing job-shop stuff, aircraft and hot rod parts. Then I decided to do wheels because I still had ideas for wheel designs that I never used at Boyds. At that time the wheels were all three-piece wheels, and I had an idea to do some two-piece wheels. And my dad and older brother were into hot rodding and I wanted to be able to make a product that they could appreciate.

Q. What are the advantages of making a wheel from billet aluminum instead of from a casting?

A. The material itself is stronger; the 6061 aluminum is very strong and it can be polished to a very bright finish. Cast wheels generally are heavier, especially the one-piece cast wheels. With billet we can create new designs faster. We have shorter R&D cycles. And billet wheels are perfectly balanced because of the precise way they are made.

Q. You make all your centers from 6061 aluminum?

A. People think we machine the centers from aluminum plate, but actually the centers are individually forged from a blank before we do any machining. We forge the centers with dies so they have most of the necessary shape, then we heat treat them to a T6 specification, and then we do the finish machining. By forging the material we make it much stronger, but it also requires less machining because the forgings already have much of the necessary shape.

Q. Are all billet wheels two-piece wheels?

A. Yes, pretty much all are two-piece wheels. The rim assembly is spun-formed from aluminum sheet and butt-fusion welded into a complete rim. We buy those complete and then press in our machined center section. After checking the runout, we weld the center section to the rim assembly.

Q. Are some billet wheels better than others, and how does the consumer tell the difference?

A. The differences are in the quality of the design, how well the manufacturer controls the runout and balance. But most of that is hard for the consumer to determine. You really have to go pretty much on the reputation of the company.

Q. How should people measure so they get the right size wheel with the right offset?

A. We tell people to call us, or visit our Web site, in order to get the instructions as to how to measure the car. If you call us we ask questions, not just about the car or its track, but things like, do you want to use disc brakes, because then you need room behind the rim for the caliper.

Q. What are the mistakes people make in buying billet wheels?

A. They buy from a company that doesn't make a quality product, which means they have runout and balance problems that the company might not stand behind. Or they buy wheels that don't provide enough room for the caliper.

Appendix

ARP
531 Spectrum Circle
Oxnard, CA 93030
800-826-3045
High-performance hardware for racing and street use

Art Morrison Enterprises
5301 8th St. E.
Fife, WA 98424
800-929-7188
Fax: 253-922-8847
www.artmorrison.com
Chassis and suspensions for drag racing and street use

Aeroquip
1695 Indian Wood Circle
Maumee, OH 43537-0700
419-891-5100
www.aeroquip.com
High-performance plumbing and fittings

Budnik Wheels
7412 Prince Dr.
Huntington Beach, CA 92647
714-848-1996
www.budnik.com
Billet wheels and accessories

Chassis Engineering
119 N. 2nd
West Branch, IA 52358
319-643-2645
www.chassisengineering.com
Chassis and suspension components for street use

Currie Enterprises
1480B N. Tustin Ave.
Anaheim, CA 92807
714-528-6957
Rear end housings, axles, components, and services

Deuce Factory
424 W. Rowland
Santa Ana, CA 92707
714-546-5596
www.deucefactory.com
*Chassis, suspension,
   and other components for 1932 Fords*

Earl's Performance Products
825 E. Sepulveda
Carson, CA 90745
213-830-1620
Performance plumbing, lines, and fittings

Engineered Components, Inc.
P.O. Box 841
Vernon, CT 06066
860-872-7046
www.ecihotrodbrakes.com
Hot rod brake components and kits

JD Squared Inc.
1601 S.W. 18th Ave.
Ocala, FL 34474
352-351-3828

Letourneau, Neal
308 Lion Lane
Shoreview, MN 55126
651-483-6958
Hot rod fabrication

Ford Motorsport SVO
Ford Motorsport Performance Equipment
44050 N. Groesbeck Highway
Clinton Township, MI 48036
Tech line: 810-468-1356
Performance equipment for Ford engines and vehicles

Heidt's Hot Rod Shop, Inc.
5420 Newport Dr. #49
Rolling Meadows, IL 60008
800-841-8188
Hot rod suspension kits and components

Kugel Komponents
451 Park Industrial Dr.
La Habra, CA 90631
562-691-7006
Hot rod suspension kits and components

Mopar Performance
248-853-7290
800-348-4696
Performance equipment for Mopar engines and vehicles

Pete and Jake's
401 Legend Lane
Peculiar, MO 64078
800-334-7240
www.peteandjakes.com
Hot rod chassis, suspensions, and other components

Phoenix Transmission Products
922 Fort Worth Hwy.
Weatherford, TX 76086
817-599-7680
Performance automatic transmissions and components

Posies
219 Duke St.
Hummelstown, PA 17036
717-566-3340
*Leaf springs, suspension kits,
  and other hot rod components*

PS Engineering
2675 Skypark Dr. #102
Torrance, CA 90505
310-534-4477
Traditional cast alloy wheels

Pure Choice Motorsports
2155 W. Acoma Blvd.
Lake Havasu City, AZ 86403
520-505-8355
Performance plumbing, lines, fittings, and kits

Richmond Gear Company
1208 Old Norris Road
Liberty, SC 29657
864-843-9231
Manual transmissions and rear end gears

Roy Brizio Street Rods
263 Wattis Way S.
San Francisco, CA 94089
650-952-7637
Hot rod chassis, components, and fabrication

Sharp Enterprises
1005 Cole St.
Laclede, MO 64651
660-963-2330
Chrome and stainless steel fasteners and hardware

SO-CAL Speed Shop
1357 Grand Ave.
Pomona, CA 91766
909-469-6171
www.so-calspeedshop.com
Hot rod chassis, components, and fabrication

Total Cost Involved
1416 W. Brooks St.
Ontario, CA 91762
909-984-1773
Hot rod chassis, suspension, and components

Wilwood
4700 Calle Bolero
Camarillo, CA 93012
805-388-1188
www.wilwood.com
Performance disc brake kits and components

Index